LIVERPOOL
world heritage city

cities500

LIVERPOOL
world heritage city
cities500

ISBN 0-9531995-8-4 (Limited Edition)
ISBN 0-9531995-6-8

Publisher: Guy Woodland
Editor-in-chief: Lew Baxter

* Guy Woodland and Lew Baxter are hereby identified as the authors of this work in accordance with section 77 of the Copyright, Design & Patents Act 1988.

Design and layout: Tynwald Creative Design
Proofreading: Judy Tasker
Partnership promotions: Marie T Vidal
Printed and bound: Bookprint SL, Barcelona, Spain

First published in 2004 by Guy Woodland
in association with *cities500*
71 Prenton Road West,
Wirral CH42 9PZ, England, UK
T: +44 (0) 151 608 7006
email: info@cities500.com
www.cities500.com

a collaboration with Barge Pole Press
www.bargepolepress.com

Introduction & Acknowledgements

It is a mark of Liverpool's astonishing renaissance in recent years that it should even be considered as a candidate for World Heritage status, that much sought after accolade bestowed by UNESCO on sites – and increasingly cities – considered of outstanding universal value. It is based on Liverpool's historic importance and its existing architectural, technological and cultural assets.

The concept of this book was inspired largely by the vision of Liverpool City Council chief executive Sir David Henshaw and council leader Mike Storey, who were determined to show that Liverpool was back on the map as a world city of stature. They pitched for European Capital of Culture for 2008. And won it. Yet in what many might have considered a 'day-dream' they had earlier put a bid together for the city to be considered a World Heritage site.

How the city's critics must have scoffed, those who for so long wrote it off as a dead end; in their jaundiced – yet mistaken – view, a former one time international maritime centre now forgotten on the far distant seaboard of Western Europe. Well, the laughter has drifted away on the Mersey's fresh breeze with UNESCO's decision to bestow that World Heritage status. Encompassed in the title *Liverpool – Maritime Mercantile City* it recognises that Liverpool is taking its rightful place as a first rank global player again.

We have to thank Sir David and Mike for their immediate encouragement for this book, at a time when the bid was still under consideration by UNESCO's eminent World Heritage Committee, and when many might have faltered at taking such a gamble. There are others who put their faith in the city and also took a gamble on the World Heritage bid being successful by supporting this book both financially and in kind.

Michael Brown, vice chancellor of Liverpool John Moores University, Drummond Bone, vice chancellor of the University of Liverpool and Gerald Pillay, rector and chief executive of Liverpool Hope University College, were the first 'partners' to come on board – and without barely drawing breath – thus demonstrating their conviction that Liverpool's past is an essential ingredient of its vibrant future; a mindset that will surely be an inspiration to the thousands of students who flock to their academic institutions from across the world. And then, there's Phil Redmond whose observations on the 'state of being a Scouser' offer a remarkable insight into the 'anything's possible' attitude of Liverpudlians.

We were thrilled that Sir Neil Cossons, chairman of English Heritage, agreed to write one of the book's foreword tributes to the city and doubly so when the Duke of Westminster agreed to write his personal commendation to the city that is embarking on the biggest regeneration programme in Europe; and under the auspices of the Duke's own Grosvenor development organisation. It goes without saying that Prime Minister Tony Blair's endorsement proves how Liverpool has arisen Phoenix-like – or rather like a Liver Bird – from the ashes of an earlier, less positive age; especially as his wife Cherie is herself a proud daughter of the city that's had its share of hurdles to clamber over.

We have had boundless help from John Hinchliffe, the World Heritage officer at Liverpool City Council, as well as encouragement from various members of the steering group assembled from a wide range of organisations to promote the bid. We were also enthused by the attitude of English Heritage in the North West of England – the city council's main advocates and advisors to the UK government on Liverpool's bid – and from Steve Broomhead, chief executive of the North West Development Agency and the organisation's marketing director Peter Mearns and media chief Emma Degg, who all unequivocally and without hesitation gave us their support and offers of help.

Indeed all of the partners, subscribers, writers, photographers and other contributors are listed in a special roll call of honour in these pages: people and organisations who declared their faith in the city's bright future, which this World Heritage status also reflects; who shared the hope, the passion and the risk, but most of all the belief that Liverpool would be elevated to this exclusive international club. Thanks also to Tony Hall for his 'picturesque' patience and help.

More than anything, though, this book is a tribute to the people of Liverpool. And apart from the photographic architectural glories of the city, we have tried to portray the wide variety of opinions, attitudes and communities – that terrific racial mélange that makes it such a fascinating, challenging place. These are compiled in a collection of essays by local writers, journalists, academics, architects and others who have a love of the city's often spiky personality. We've also included a number of profiles of individual people whose lives and relevance to the city are an essential ingredient of Liverpool's cultural legacy. These are stories about and by people who have been captivated by this remarkable city: their observations and occasionally perceptive commentaries on its vagaries. In this way, the book is more than a photographic record; it is a work of contemporary observation.

And, finally, we are delighted that part of the proceeds of this book are to be donated to the performing arts bursary that will help aspiring young students from disadvantaged communities in Liverpool's inner city and London's Camden area; a charitable trust set up to commemorate Greg Greenidge, a Liverpool man who devoted a large part of his tragically short life to racial harmony and who was so utterly disdainful of narrow minded prejudice. He was, as his mother explains further in these pages, a steadying, calming influence on family, friends and all of those who had the good fortune to come within his circle.

Lew Baxter and Guy Woodland

July 2004

Contributors

Photography

Guy Woodland

Steve Dodd
Ron Jones
Angela Hurren
Anthony McArdle
Hal Mullin
Henry Woodland
Liverpool City Council

Photos pages 159, 177, 209 & 229
courtesy of Liverpool Daily Post & Echo

Writers

Lew Baxter

Will Alsop
Stephen Binns
Drummond Bone
Michael Brown
Sue Carmichael
Laura Davis
Jim Gill
Peter Grant
Saranda Hajdari
John Hinchliffe
Adrian Jarvis
Phil Key
Ann Lodge
Arabella McIntyre-Brown
Gerald John Pillay
Phil Redmond
Joe Riley
Barbara Smith
Ian Wray

Celebratory Partners

Leading Partners

Liverpool John Moores University
The University of Liverpool
Liverpool Hope University College
Liverpool City Council
Mersey Television
The North West Development Agency
The Paradise Street Project (Grosvenor)

•

Ethel Austin
Downing Developments

•

Liverpool Chamber of Commerce

•

The Mersey Partnership
Urban Splash

•

Rathbone Investment Management Ltd
Davies Wallis Foyster (DWF)
Mercer Human Resource Consulting Limited
Purcell Miller Triton
PricewaterhouseCoopers LLP
Kaleidoscope ADM
Living Ventures

Contents

1O DOWNING STREET
LONDON SW1A 2AA

Foreword by

Tony Blair
The Prime Minister

Liverpool is a vibrant city. It continues to flourish as a resonant and resourceful place and owes much of its regeneration and success to the spirit and tenacity of the people in its communities. The city's rich maritime history has left a legacy of historic docks, cultural buildings and collections including one of the finest, and most complete, Victorian commercial districts in Britain. The outstanding universal value of this legacy has now been formally recognised with the inscription of *Liverpool – Maritime Mercantile City* on the list of World Heritage sites. This is a remarkable achievement by everyone who worked towards the goal of becoming the United Kingdom's 26th World Heritage site.

The Government attaches great importance to the value of our historic environment. The photographs and essays in this book portray much of the richness of Liverpool's own heritage that will continue to be valued and enjoyed by generations to come.

Tony Blair

World Heritage Committee

Suzhou, China: 28 June–7 July 2004

According to UNESCO's heritage chief Francesco Bandarin, China's lovely Suzhou gardens are truly representative of eastern gardens and are one of the main inspirations for gardens worldwide.

Located in east China's Jiangsu Province, Suzhou was the venue for the 28th Conference of the UNESCO's World Heritage Committee. The city, just south of the Yangtze River delta and not far from Taihu Lake is also famed for its jade carvings and silk embroidery.

The site of the city dates back almost 3,000 years and it was named Suzhou in the 7th century AD. Long considered a tourist attraction the Venetian traveller and explorer Marco Polo also stayed there at one point.

The history of Suzhou's fabled gardens can also be traced back over 2500 years ago; at one point there was more than 100 spectacular gardens and nine of them have been designated World Heritage sites in their own right.

Once purely the domain of the rich and powerful, the gardens are now enjoyed by all the citizens and visitors to this captivating centre, which also boasts a network of canals, and is nicknamed the Venice of the East.

Seventy of the original gardens have been preserved, among them the inspiring 'Master-of-Nets' garden with its unique evening time display that emphasises the tranquillity of the setting, enhanced by the mellow music of the region. During the past two years, Suzhou has expanded its attractions even further by laying out another 100 small gardens, each covering around 500 square metres with pavilions, trees, ponds and rockery.

The city itself has been transformed into an Oriental visual delight, after a refurbishment programme where buildings have been painted and restored. City officials have also launched a US$723 million heritage protection programme, mainly to divert water from the Taihu Lake and the Yangtze River to replenish the waterway systems of the old town.

News of World Heritage success reaches Liverpool's municipal headquarters.

**Eaton Hall
Chester
CH4 9ET**

Foreword by

His Grace the Duke of Westminster

Even a decade ago if Liverpool had considered bidding for World Heritage status it would surely have been dismissed as far too ambitious. It is a striking indication of how far the city has travelled in radically changing its image that no one is really surprised that it did so and has achieved its aim.

There is little doubt this is probably one of the most exciting and important decisions to affect Liverpool since King John bestowed on it the charter of city eight centuries ago. Further, it has international significance for people across the world.

The accolade of World Heritage status underlines the city's remarkable social, commercial and cultural renaissance in contemporary times; overshadowing even its epic maritime history.

I am doubly pleased, as Grosvenor is embarking on the largest and most dynamic regeneration construction programme in Liverpool's history with the exciting Paradise Street Development. This scheme will transform the face of the city centre and cement the building blocks of Liverpool's future aspirations.

Foreword by

Sir Neil Cossons
Chairman of English Heritage

The decision by UNESCO to confer World Heritage status on Liverpool confirms what English Heritage, Liverpool City Council and the people of Liverpool have always known – it is beyond question one of the great cities of the world. Liverpool's historic buildings are instantly recognisable and are a proud reminder that this was a hugely important maritime and mercantile city on the world stage; gateway to the new world, Liverpool was the greatest seaport of the old.

Today we see Liverpool's future intimately bound up with the celebration of its distinguished past. 21st century Liverpool is undergoing an extraordinary period of development that will change the way the city looks forever. It is only right, therefore, that Britain's world-famous industrial past be recognised, preserved and protected as the city embraces the great opportunities for regeneration and prosperity. However, it is our duty to ensure that we do not unknowingly lose the very things that make Liverpool special.

All great cities go through cycles of growth, decay, and hopefully revival. Liverpool's acknowledged decline in the latter part of the 20th century has been reversed through a vigorous and enthusiastic renaissance that is being driven by all of its citizens and those who realise its potential.

At the core of this vigour is a powerful realisation that the legacy of the city's distinguished past provides the key to an equally distinguished and perhaps even more vibrant future. As England's finest Victorian city Liverpool enjoys a unique opportunity to honour its great architectural heritage by finding new uses for its eminent buildings. And the city can further endorse that inheritance by setting superlative standards for the new.

World Heritage status focuses attention on the need to manage change carefully and to take advantage of the enormous asset that the city's historic environment affords us.

Neil Cossons

Mike Storey CBE
Leader of
Liverpool City Council

Britain could not have a more deserving World Heritage site. It is an accolade the city deserves. There are few examples of architecture in the world that can match Liverpool's imposing waterfront and its cultural buildings. Liverpool is truly the 'World in One City', and this is reflected in its rich architectural legacy.

Liverpool is enjoying growth undreamed of 20 years ago. The people of Liverpool have been determined to see their city transformed – economically, socially and image-wise. Liverpool has always been a city which looks outwards. World Heritage status is global recognition of that.

But it is not just about looking to our past. It is about looking to Liverpool's place in the world today – a confident, thriving and ambitious premier European city, known and respected throughout the world.

Sir David Henshaw
Chief Executive
Liverpool City Council

Confidence in Liverpool is higher than it has been in living memory.

Liverpool's historic waterfront and the magnificent architectural legacy of the cultural and business quarters have long held local people, commerce and visitors from across the world in their thrall. But this magnificent area of the city is not here just to admire – it is helping drive the city's regeneration

UNESCO's World Heritage status is a tribute to our remarkable past as well as a platform for our exciting future. It will power Liverpool's transformation into a vibrant and modern world class city.

Thus, the remarkable economic and social regeneration of Liverpool over recent years, combined with European Capital of Culture in 2008, and now World Heritage Status, establishes the city as a formidable, global player.

This is an extraordinary, incredible period in Liverpool's history that will change the city forever.

World Heritage

World Heritage sites are selected by the World Heritage committee according to the provisions of the 1972 convention of the United Nations Educational, Scientific and Cultural Organisation (UNESCO).

There are natural World Heritage sites, which are outstanding examples of geology, ecology, natural beauty or natural habitats, such as the Great Barrier Reef and the Grand Canyon.

There are also cultural World Heritage sites' which include outstanding examples of monuments or groups of buildings such as the Great Wall of China, the Pyramids and the Taj Mahal.

But there is a growing awareness that the world's most important cultural heritage is not restricted to ancient civilisations. Mankind has had a greater impact on the environment in the last 200 years than in all of its previous occupation of the planet; and the most impressive creations from this period are as important as any that came before them.

From the late 18th century until the early 20th century, the United Kingdom was the foremost industrial nation in the world, and has an industrial heritage that is of unique international significance.

Liverpool's integral – even pioneering – role in the Industrial Revolution involved incredible human achievement in commerce, technology and architecture, and it made a major contribution to Britain's worldwide dominance of industry in the Victorian era. It is, therefore, fitting that it should now be recognised for that astonishing legacy.

The World Heritage committee's elite 21 members represent the 172 nations and states that are party to the global convention for the universal protection of mankind's cultural and national heritage. It currently protects more than 750 worldwide sites of 'outstanding universal value'.

English Heritage

It is the job of English Heritage to make sure that the historic environment of England is properly maintained and cared for. The organisation employs some of the country's very best architects, archaeologists and historians, and aims to help people understand and appreciate why the historic buildings and landscapes around them matter. From the first traces of civilisation, to the most significant buildings of the 20th century, it believes that every important historic site should get the care and attention it deserves.

Liverpool Maritime Mercantile City

World Heritage – the key areas that fall within the site:

- **The Waterfront:** incorporating the Pier Head and the Albert Dock conservation area.
- **The Greater Waterfront:** taking in the Stanley Dock conservation area.
- **The Business Centre:** traversing the Castle Street, Dale Street and Old Hall Street commercial areas.
- **The Cultural Quarter:** spanning William Brown Street and encompassing St George's Hall and the splendour of Liverpool Museum and the Walker Art Gallery, along with the William Brown Library.
- **The Cultural Living Area:** revolving around Lower Duke Street in what is now becoming the city's new cultural hot-spot.
- **City Buffer Zone:** a specially designated buffer zone has also been established to protect the visual setting of the specified World Heritage site.

The Waterfront
zones 1 & 2

'... the prospect of turning the overwhelming tide of neglect and negativism seemingly almost insurmountable, [but] Liverpool still held a magnetic attraction, and we stayed on ...'

Sue Carmichael

see essay page 84

The Port of Liverpool –
the Maritime Gateway to the World

by Adrian Jarvis

The fortunes of Liverpool are inextricably linked with the fortunes of its port. If the mid 1980s were the city's darkest hour, so too were they the nadir of the Mersey Docks & Harbour Company's effort to turn round a port which had been in rapid and seemingly irreversible decline since the late 1960s. The accelerating rise in the prosperity and self-confidence of the city which followed has been synchronised with the success of the port's efforts.

It has long been so. In the late 17th century, when Liverpool began its long rise from obscurity, it was a growth of trade on the river – estuarine, sea-going and trans-Atlantic – which fuelled it. Crucially, the town was home to a forceful little merchant community who determined that some of the proceeds should be reinvested to foster continued growth. In 1715, Liverpool opened the first commercial wet dock in the world and from the 1720s onwards it consistently pursued improved access to the hinterland, becoming involved along the way in the promotion of the first industrial canal in the world, the Sankey Navigation, opened in 1757. The Sankey and its rival the Douglas Navigation, made coal reasonably cheaply available on the Mersey, which, together with improved berthing for vessels and marking of the channels, made Liverpool attractive to a number of industries which involved moving heavy low-value goods around, including salt refining, copper smelting and pottery.

The estuarine and coastwise vessels which brought the raw materials and took away the products produced profits for their owners, for the manufacturers and for the port authority. That in turn made further investment in port improvement possible. It started gently, with minor improvements to the Old Dock and its approaches but by the time Salthouse Dock was opened in 1753 the pace was gathering: it took 38 years to need the first extra dock but only 22 to need the next, seven the next – and they were getting bigger as well. This is not the place to list all the docks, but perhaps it is the place to mention that in 1848 five new docks were opened on the same day.

This continuing investment in docks was essential: the Mersey is a hostile river; especially for small sailing vessels before steam tugs became available. But once that investment was made, Liverpool's good canal connections with Lancashire, Yorkshire and Cheshire together with her extensive coastwise fleet made it the most effective and sought-after port on the west coast. When Bristol eventually bestirred itself and

invested it was already too late. The Liverpool dog had not only seen the rabbit, he was already washing up after having cooked and eaten it. The form of the metaphorical meal was the Liverpool Improvement Act of 1786.

Mid 18th century Liverpool was a boomtown, buoyed along with the steady profits of its routine imports such as timber and its exports of manufactured goods, sometimes boosted by spectacular bonuses from slave trading and privateering. But there is a downside to being a boomtown, which is that too many people are trying to live in too small a space, resulting not just in overcrowding but also in hideously insanitary conditions. The 1786 Improvement Act was almost a proto-town planning act, stipulating maximum heights of buildings and minimum clearances between them. It paved and lit the streets and it did away with such necessities of Georgian elegance as streetside slaughterhouses. But it did it at great civic expense, and the eventual come-back was the Bolton case of 1833, when a group of merchants declined to pay the Town Dues on the grounds that they were a local tax on shipping and hence their proceeds should be spent on the port. Thirteen archive boxes full of legal proceedings later, it was ruled that the Corporation could use the Town Dues for the improvement of the town, thus cementing the relationship between the respective fortunes of the town and the port.

Naturally, improvements went in cycles, and those of 1786 were soon engulfed in another excess of population. Even the first cholera pandemic of 1832 failed to solve the problem, because not enough people died of it to reduce the population density to acceptable limits or to deter in-migrants. A more humane alternative was to make the town habitable by more people, and two decisive steps were taken in 1846 with the appointment of the country's first medical officer of health and the first borough

Dr Adrian Jarvis is currently co-director of the Centre for Port & Maritime History at the Merseyside Maritime Museum. He was appointed 'trainee in shipping' at the City of Liverpool Museums in 1968 and has worked for the museums in various capacities ever since. In 1988 he took a completely new turn, into researching the history of the Port of Liverpool, using the Maritime Museum's wonderful Mersey Docks & Harbour Board archive. He flies the flag for Liverpool on the international conference circuit and has served two terms as secretary-general of the International Commission for Maritime History. He has published extensively and has hosted several international conferences in Liverpool. The Centre for Port & Maritime History is a partnership between National Museums Liverpool and the University of Liverpool, which is currently engaged in a large and groundbreaking research project investigating the late 19th century merchant community of Liverpool. Dr Jarvis is unusual in holding honorary appointments in two different faculties of the university, namely arts and engineering.

engineer. Dr Duncan's job was to find the causes of disease and James Newlands' job was to remove them. At the time they were appointed, conditions were already back to (at best) 1786 standards, and the town would very shortly be overwhelmed by huge numbers of starving Irish fleeing the potato famine. How could the town progress?

The answer lay in its trade, which by this time was not only large and lucrative, but also incredibly broad-based. 1848 was a catastrophic year in which several European countries had revolutions, the railway mania collapsed, the cotton trade was in severe difficulties, the Bank of England was leaking gold at an unsustainable level and several parliamentary inquiries failed to find a solution. It was also the year that Liverpool opened five new docks. They did so on borrowed money, and it is incredible, but true, that in 1848 the Liverpool Dock Trustees were better able to borrow money than was the Bank of England. That was because, if your trade was sufficiently broad-based, every cloud had a silver lining. It was a bad year in cotton, but an excellent one in timber, and the stoppage of railway construction works produced a surplus of railway line, which could be bought for cheap and sold very profitably in the USA. Even the Irish paupers who arrived in Liverpool had not walked here: somebody had profited from their misery by selling them a ferry ticket.

In some ways, this was the pinnacle of the port's fortunes. There's a very old joke to the effect that Merseyside has the two best football teams in the country – Liverpool and Liverpool Reserves. In the 1840s, Liverpool had the two best dock engineers in the

The 60-metre square-rigged brigantine sts Prince William *'heaves her head round' at the start of the Mersey River Festival, summer 2004. She is one of two owned by the Tall Ships Youth Trust, and has a crew of 65, including 48 trainees.*

world – Jesse Hartley and his son and deputy, John. By 1860, the two of them had designed and built a string of new docks, each bigger than the last, such as the world had never seen before.

In the mid 50s another attempt, this time partially successful, was made to drive a wedge between the town and its port. It came from an unholy alliance between Manchester and Wirral and eventually resulted in the largest and most successful single port authority in the world having to take over the dog's breakfast of incompetent engineering and corrupt financing known as Birkenhead Docks, and eventually being dispossessed of the Liverpool system in which they and their forebears had prudently invested. The Mersey Docks & Harbour Board Act 1857 was a truly outrageous piece of legislation.

The port survived it: despite being forced to spend millions on the proven failure at Birkenhead and forbidden to spend money on the proven success in Liverpool, still it survived and grew. How much better it might have done without the intrusion of the government is open to speculation.

It now sustained two further heavy blows: Jesse Hartley was a very old man, and early in 1860 he retired (at the age of 80) and died shortly afterwards. John succeeded him, but after 15 months he was forced into retirement by ill health. His successor was George Fosbery Lyster, who was clearly very able but not in the Hartley league, and he represented a break with a tradition extending back to 1824. Work was no longer got right first time, involving some very expensive reconstructions, which added to the port's interest costs without adding proportionately to its income. In particular, a huge (£4.1 million) programme of works under an Act of 1873 was only partly successful, needing updating under two major programmes of works from 1891–1901 and 1898–1908.

These problems were largely hidden, because the trade of the port continued to increase by leaps and bounds. The problem was that, while in the past it had been not merely surpassing competitors but completely out-distancing them, now it was now sucked back into competition with ports like Bristol or Manchester which it could formerly afford to regard with complete disdain. Soon, this relative decline would be out in the open.

When Liverpool celebrated its 700th anniversary in 1907, the wiser heads in the city were already aware that the shipping industry in general, and Liverpool's in particular, was not in a strong or stable condition. But this was known only to a few insiders, and to the rest of the population, which had reached 684,947 at the 1901 Census, everything seemed wonderful. The city centre was being transformed by the building of prestige office blocks and the population density of the inner parts of the city was being reduced by the rapid spread of electric tramways. Symbolising it all was the magnificent newly-completed Dock Offices building at the Pier Head: the source of a worldwide business (illustrated in the stained glass of the light wells) in which one-seventh of the world's shipping tonnage was owned in Liverpool. The huge new liner *Lusitania* brought the Blue Riband of the Atlantic back where it belonged, and the previous year the Dock Board had received Parliamentary authority to build a new dock of unprecedented size and depth to accommodate ships up to 50% bigger even than her. The labour force of the Dock Engineer's department is said to have peaked at 11,000, and the Board's income from rates and dues ran at around £1.3 million per year.

The Great War did not change all that, or at least not immediately, because it was easier to defend merchant shipping using west coast ports than east coast ones, and the immediate aftermath of war saw a huge boom in shipping and shipbuilding, with the Board's income reaching an unprecedented £2.6 million in 1920. It couldn't last, and many shipping firms soon found themselves in difficulty through over-investing in new ships while scarcity prices prevailed. There were some spectacular collapses, of which the greatest was Royal Mail Lines, a huge group with interests in virtually every major

Renovations and piling in the Albert Dock, 1984.

shipping route. It took a number of Liverpool companies down with it, including Elder Dempster and White Star. Despite the economic mayhem surrounding it, the port recorded a new record tonnage in 1930: these were very trying times for the Board and some desperate economy measures were needed, but they survived the Depression surprisingly well. This was in part another case of the benefits of diversity: during this period the bulk grain trade grew enormously, helping fill the trade gap left by the lamentable state of the cotton trade. There cannot have been many companies that posted record profits in 1932, but the Liverpool Grain Storage and Transit Company was one of them.

The stories of the Blitz and the Battle of the Atlantic are well known and need no re-telling here, but their aftermath is another matter. The shipping and shipbuilding industries soon embarked on what became known as 'the long boom', but the ports industry generally was not invited to the party. The Port of Liverpool had struggled desperately to keep itself open, but it had built up arrears of maintenance during the pre-war economies and was now faced with a vast amount of reconstruction and modernisation. Over two linear miles of transit sheds had been destroyed, warehouses at Wapping, Albert and Stanley had been seriously damaged, most of the floating plant was in poor condition and the Dock Yard had been hit as well, damaging the capacity to repair other things. There were serious arrears of dredging. The financial situation seemed sound, with dues passing the £5 million mark in 1950, but it was not sufficient for the task, and the proportion of income swallowed up by debt charges rose inexorably.

The city faced similar problems, but with an added twist of the screw. the condition of much of its infrastructure (especially the tram system) was poor, the perennial slum problem had been made far worse by the loss of housing stock destroyed and some of the finest municipal buildings, including the Library, the Museum and St George's Hall had been heavily damaged. The added twist was that the immediate pre-war years had seen the start of the move of industries to the edge of, and often beyond, the city boundary, which diminished the 'product of a penny rate', and this continued, most conspicuously with the handing over of the huge Royal Ordnance Factory at Kirkby to become a large industrial estate.

The port struggled, but survived, and the late 1950s and early '60s saw new records of tonnage and revenue. Some major projects of modernisation were achieved, including the new Waterloo Entrance for the coastwise and short-sea trades in general and 'Irish Boats' in particular. Contrary to popular belief, the Dock Board was not caught napping by the onrush of containerisation: it had an interim facility in service in 1968 and a very substantial permanent one – Royal Seaforth – under construction. It was now that the millstones of debt began to bear down on the Board, and they combined with government vacillations over whether or not to nationalise the independent ports to bring about a complete financial collapse, necessitating a huge rescue operation and the reconstruction of the Board as a Company.

Before that happened, the Board had already made the decision to close all the docks upstream of Pier Head, implemented in 1972. This came as a terrible culture shock to people in Liverpool. The south docks were home to household names like Elder Dempster, Harrison's and Guinness: their closure seemed inconceivable. But the Board was right: even in the early days of containerisation, one container ship did the work of about eight conventional cargo liners and the ratio was rising fast. The best parts of the south docks – those modernised between 1898 and 1908 – could not handle ships of the size now anticipated and furthermore they were the wrong shape. What was needed now was fewer berths and more open ground for stacking and handling containers. A million or two square feet of useless transit sheds stood in the way.

There was another problem too: when the new Brunswick Entrances were opened in 1905, they had been built on the assumption that recent huge improvements in dredging technology would allow the maintenance of a dredged channel through the Pluckington Bank. One might as well have threatened the Kray brothers with a water pistol: the maintenance of an adequate approach to the south docks remained a crippling expense until their closure. This was the turning point: when the south docks sank they took a lot with them in the shape of businesses serving the ships, from grocers to chandlers to lifeboat repairers. Closure followed swiftly for such railway depots as still survived. Even the pubs were massacred: where there were literally dozens, just two survive today. Hundreds of acres stood derelict, and they mostly did so in a very conspicuous way. The MD&HC had no funds to invest – it was still fighting for its life – and the City Council was no better placed. Private redevelopment proposals mainly centred on the area from Pier Head to Albert and all but one of them promised wholesale destruction. After all, 'everybody knew' that it was impossible to redevelop old docks encumbered with derelict buildings, dubious retaining walls and anything up to 10 metres of mildly toxic silt.

If it is true, as is popularly believed, that the redevelopment of the south docks was largely driven by the intervention of Michael Heseltine as

The majestic QE2 *attracts the crowds along the Wirral waterfront on her visit to Liverpool in May 2004.*

'Minister for Merseyside' and the Merseyside Development Corporation, but it is worth reminding the reader that the first small piece of redevelopment was the Pilot Phase of Merseyside Maritime Museum, opened in 1980 by the largely forgotten and generally unloved Merseyside County Council. That tiny success proved the point: people would visit dead docks, and if they would do it to visit a museum, why should they not do it for shopping, for food and drink, for other forms of entertainment? Hell, it was even possible they might live there.

I do not know who coined the expression 'Merseypride', but the sentiment clearly existed in the days of Jesse Hartley and GF Lyster. In an age when corporate offices were rare, the Traffic Office at Albert was built with a Tuscan portico of cast iron. Where a wooden hut would have done to protect the gatemen at the river entrances, beautiful little granite houses, a stonemason's *tour de force,* were built instead. They are to remind the visitor, whether from the landward or the seaward side that this is Liverpool, where the port authority does things properly. At both the north and the south extremities of the World Heritage site there is a granite pumping station and accumulator tower in neo-medieval style, while at Canning half-tide there is a brick one with pressed brick and terracotta enhancements, to say nothing of some very fancy brickwork on the chimney. The corn warehouses at Waterloo were, rightly, taken seriously as a piece of architecture, despite their mundane function. They, too, may have turned out that way as an expression of power, but perhaps there was more to it than that.

The old port buildings surviving in the World Heritage site reflect the attitude of their designers and their 'political' masters. Among the conditions of the architectural competition for the 1907 Dock Offices we find the words '... it shall be dignified as befits its purpose'. That is the extra dimension: structures were dignified to express the pride the members of the port authority felt in their role, the pride the engineers felt in their design and the pride the craftsmen felt in being given quality materials with which to do a quality job that they probably fully expected still to be there in 150 years.

Over the centuries, Liverpool has invested a lot of pride in its port: with a slight semantic shift, the World Heritage site marks payback time, when the history of the port will invest Liverpool with pride.

World Heritage –
the Winning Case for Liverpool

by John Hinchliffe

There is no doubt that the decision of UNESCO (the United Nations Educational, Scientific and Cultural Organisation) is a major coup for Liverpool, especially as World Heritage is considered to be the 'Oscars' of the heritage accolades. Unless the city is engulfed in an unexpected catastrophic environmental disaster this status will last in perpetuity.

The inscription process began almost five years ago when Liverpool was put on the tentative list being drawn up by the UK government's department for culture, media and sport. They were considering which UK sites might meet UNESCO's strict criteria for World Heritage site status.

Many wondered if Liverpool, which many may consider to be simply an old industrial seaport, had the right credentials. However, English Heritage, the government's heritage advisors, had recognised that there was a changing perspective in UNESCO's thinking. They wanted to try and broaden the type and distribution of sites. Traditionally World Heritage sites had tended to focus on 'ancient' and 'monumental' sites but UNESCO had recognised that mankind has had a greater influence on the environment in the last 200 years than at any time previously and wanted to increase the number of sites from that period.

There was a two-fold shift in emphasis, with a move to increase the number of sites in other parts of the world – as there has been a slight dominance of Europe on the World Heritage list – and to inscribe sites that are a result in some form or other of the Industrial Revolution. UNESCO had also indicated it was keen to look at the historic environment as a whole rather than just individual buildings or monuments. English Heritage has also reflected that change with its *Power of Place (2000)* proposals and by the British government with its *Force For Our Future (2001)* agenda, both significant policy documents driven by the desire to take an holistic overview.

Indeed, the UK government is currently engaged in a *Heritage Protection Review,* a study of how we should protect our historic environment, including listed buildings, conservation areas, ancient monuments, historic parks and gardens and historic battlefields. Rather than just considering individual buildings or areas, the current emphasis is on looking at the management of the whole of the environment. The recent inscription of the extensive Derwent Valley Mills World Heritage site and the Liverpool bid are clearly in line with that developing conservation policy.

The reality of Liverpool's bid was that it needed extensive research and no one really thought the nomination could be submitted before the middle of 2004. I took up this post in the late summer of 2001 with a brief to shape the nomination and assemble a steering group that would drive the bid. Within weeks of arriving I was told that there was a marvellous window of opportunity for Liverpool to submit a bid by January 2003. I must admit I was surprised and a little taken aback. We had a year to tackle what we expected to be a two and half year programme.

English Heritage and Liverpool city council agreed that Liverpool should attempt this, as it was very much aware of a critical change in UNESCO guidelines. Previously the World Heritage committee had accepted as many nominations as came forward, but in an attempt to restrict bids from countries that already boasted a substantial number of sites it was decreed that they should only be allowed one every year.

At the time there was no other location in Britain quite ready to take up that January 2003 option. We realised if we could get our act together by the beginning of the year there was a strong possibility that Liverpool could be the UK inscription in 2004. We looked at the task before us and decided to go that extra mile, and in virtually half the time. We are actually 18 months ahead of our original schedule, a demonstration of the new 'can do' attitude that is pervading Liverpool.

English Heritage had drawn up a draft outline of the Liverpool site for inclusion in the government's tentative list and that was refined following a more detailed study and a deeper examination of what constitutes Liverpool's outstanding universal value. The most significant change to the original site was the inclusion of the William Brown Street cultural quarter. This additional area was included because its outstanding architecture and the remarkable collections in the Walker art gallery, the

John Hinchliffe is originally from West Yorkshire but studied planning at the University of Manchester and conservation at the University of Central Lancashire. He is a member of the Royal Town Planning Institute and the Institute of Historic Buildings Conservation, as well as The Georgian Group, The Victorian Society, The National Trust, Merseyside Civic Society and Lathom Park Trust. John has lived in a Georgian townhouse in Liverpool city centre for over 20 years, where he has received daily inspiration from the dominant presence of Giles Gilbert Scott's Anglican Cathedral. Prior to his current post of World Heritage officer for Liverpool city council, which he took up in August 2001, he worked as conservation officer in Wirral and West Lancashire, where his major achievements were saving many derelict buildings from demolition and collapse by taking a proactive approach to Buildings at Risk. As World Heritage officer for Liverpool he coordinated the compiling of the UNESCO bid nomination document, winning support from the government's department of media, culture and sport.

Museum and the Central Library are a symbol of tremendous civic pride, funded by the maritime mercantile trade. St George's Hall is, of course, widely accepted as one of the finest neo-classical buildings in the world.

We were also influenced by the presence of Lime Street station, the great point of arrival for generations of emigrants and one end of the historically important Liverpool and Manchester Railway – a pioneering part of the transport network revolution that was vital for carrying export and import goods like cotton, wool, coal, salt and iron, feeding and being fed by the river Mersey and the port.

A steering group consisting of representatives of national, regional and local organisations was set up to guide the bid. I am especially grateful the to North West Development Agency for its financial assistance, which enabled us to produce high quality documentation. The people of Liverpool were consulted regularly, with a series of information bulletins asking for their opinions and their support for the bid. We were encouraged that there was almost universal enthusiasm from everyone consulted.

The theme of the bid was 'Liverpool – the supreme example of a commercial port at the time of Britain's greatest global influence'. Of course some people were confused that we hadn't included Liverpool's grandiose cathedrals in the bid, despite them being two of the 20th century's greatest buildings. We were aware that medieval European cathedrals already dominate the World Heritage list and considered that they didn't fit neatly into the overall theme of Liverpool's bid.

Copies of Liverpool's World Heritage bid document were stored in a traditional nautical chest in the city council's offices.

There were similar strong suggestions, with some validity we thought, for including the Canning area, largely because of its extensive spread of Georgian and 19th century houses. We reluctantly cast against this as most are already protected under statutory British conservation laws and we were aware that in the UK two of the existing World Heritage sites are the city of Bath and the city of Edinburgh, both representing similar styles of Georgian housing.

On a personal level I am delighted to have been a part of the team that has been able to bring World Heritage status to my adopted city. I am from Yorkshire originally – born in a small town between Leeds and Huddersfield – but in the last 25 years Liverpool has been my home and it has given me great joy.

There is a delicious irony that whereas Heathcliffe – from Charlotte Bronte's *Wuthering Heights* – was first a foundling on the streets of Liverpool and transported to the wild moors of Yorkshire where he wrought such havoc, I have come from that very same Bronte country, but hope I've had a much more beneficial impact on Liverpool's future. I am proud to be able to give something back to this marvellous city.

In effect there are four principal benefits of becoming a World Heritage site: there is the international acknowledgement of Liverpool's importance in world history, but also of its surviving architectural and technological heritage; and secondly there is the image of the city. There is no denying that over the years we've have some pretty bad press. Now we've already noticed that winning European Capital of Culture has changed that image for the better. In changing the image of the city it will attract more tourists and business investment. There is also the advantage that with World Heritage under out belt there is increased access to grant aid, the higher the heritage accolade, the more chance of funding for various projects. Finally, of course, it is a matter of ensuring that the site overall is managed properly in the future. We have produced a management plan – guided by UNESCO's requirements – that encompasses a wide range of issues that affect the site.

People assume that having World Heritage status is about conserving buildings but it is much more than that; it is about achieving an appropriate and equitable balance between conservation and regeneration. It is a matter of promoting future development of the right type and scale, and in the right place. More than even that, it is about promoting a proper understanding of Liverpool's World Heritage site, about interpreting the special qualities of the city and helping visitors to understand its fabulous legacy and history.

In terms of future ideas, such as Will Alsop's proposals for the Pier Head, a lot depends on how World Heritage values are defined. In our nomination statement we made it clear that one of Liverpool's merits has been its spirit of innovation over the years. That was proved long ago with the Leeds and Liverpool canal system, the construction of the railway links with Manchester, the early docks, and its trail-blazing road tunnel under the river, along with plenty of buildings that demonstrate this willingness to harness new technology and building styles. We feel that in allowing a new innovative building concept such as the Fourth Grace, we are continuing that spirit. It is important to point out that Liverpool is an evolving, growing and living city; and cities like this must continue to have new buildings.

Liverpool was not built in just one period and is not comprised of structures of one particular type; it boasts grand buildings from the early 18th century through to the mid 20th century and we are merely striving to continue that tradition. It is a matter of having something that is exciting and daring, rather than safe, boring and bland. We believe we can make a strong case for allowing an iconic building on that Fourth Grace site.

Of course, now that we are an inscribed World Heritage site planning is a material consideration in the determination of planning applications. Anyone who is proposing developments within the site *per se,* or even the buffer zone, must comply with the objectives that are defined in our World Heritage Management Plan, and we hope to be able to raise standards of architecture, urban design and building conservation.

The buffer zone is intended to protect the visual setting of the World Heritage site proper and adopts the same concept as with listed buildings and conservation areas, where there is a statutory requirement to consider the impact of development proposals on their setting. The buffer zone provides an additional area of interest as it shows there are interesting elements beyond the World Heritage boundary, and it takes in many of the interesting aspects of the city.

World Heritage site status will not impose any further statutory constraints upon architects and builders as those controls are already in place by virtue of the existing British planning system. The fundamental vision of the new status is to ensure that the site is managed as an exemplary demonstration of sustainable development and heritage-led regeneration.

The imposing 'crown' of
the Metropolitan Cathedral
of Christ the King
overlooks the original
clock tower of the
University of Liverpool's
Victoria Building, which
was designed by local
architect Alfred Waterhouse
and built in red pressed
brick. It opened in 1892.

'Of course I have
this ongoing love affair
with Liverpool,
in spite of my
seeming fury at
its apparent disorder.'

Ken Martin

see essay page 222

Tracing the Roots of Liverpool's Past

There are elements of Liverpool's murky past that were suppressed from the public consciousness for many, many decades: its involvement – perhaps even significant role – in the invidious slave trade in the 18th century in particular was rarely mentioned, indeed was glossed over.

They too are an important part of the cultural and heritage legacy that makes the city what it is today: especially with the general acknowledgement of that shameful period in the city's history. It is known that about a quarter of Liverpool's shipping fleet were slavers, although there may have been no slave ships actually berthing in the Mersey as the trade was mostly outward from West Africa to America. Yet there were certainly some slaves sold here: auctioned in coffee houses, shops and warehouses, even on the steps of the Custom House. And the shipowners did make fortunes: the first slave ship out of the Mersey was the *Liverpool Merchant* – her cargo of 220 Africans was sold in Barbados in the 1740s. The last slave ship with 'a Liverpool registration' was the *Kitty Amelia* in 1807. It is estimated that, of the two million slaves transported from West Africa, fewer than half survived the horrors of conditions at sea, or the brutality and disease they suffered later.

Many of those links with Liverpool have been brought to light – often in an emotionally painful way for the descendants of those savagely treated men and women – thanks to a 'walking tour' established by the proudly black Liverpudlian, Eric Lynch, whose own family came from Barbados, ironically, to live in the city that had played a part in the callous devastation of their original communities.

Now 72 and a respected local historian, albeit amateur, Eric first became aware of the issues connecting Liverpool to slavery when he taught himself to read and write at 16. One of the first books he read was Ramsey Muir's ancient history of Liverpool, moved in particular by a chapter on the vast fortunes that Liverpool made on the back of the slave trade, quite literally. It stirred in him the zeal to find out more about the past of his ancestors. Over his years as a city council employee in the building department, he had continually hammered home the race awareness message – to such an extent that eventually he helped set up a series of formal courses that put the spotlight on race and equality. They were a huge success and in his spare time, at weekends and in the evenings, Eric gradually expanded this into the development of what he now terms the *Slavery History* tours. His 'walks' have become almost a part of urban folklore, as he wanders over the city pointing out the relevance of buildings and streets and their connections to the slave trade. They attract locals, keen finally to face the reality, or visitors from across the UK and elsewhere, many sometimes quite emotionally affected by the historical facts.

Eric, who works closely with the University of Liverpool's *Black Roots* summer school, conducts the tours mostly at weekends with his friend and colleague Dorothy Kuya, who is equally fervent about revealing the truth of the evil practices of yesteryear. They have had such an impact on people seeking to check out their origins that a television crew from Barbados has made a documentary film, based on Eric's observations and findings, which was broadcast all over the Caribbean.

A World-class University
in a World-class City

by Professor Michael Brown

At the beginning of the 1990s, the Liverpool John Moores University (JMU) Trust Office published a report on the economic impact of higher education in Liverpool. The Trust's research revealed that during term time there were over 50,000 students living and working in the city and that one in four young people was identified as studying in full-time further or higher education. The report changed the way in which education was viewed in Liverpool, and the city's universities were finally credited as a major contributing force in the economy.

Education has always been a driving force in Liverpool, a catalyst for change and improvement, and this stretches beyond the business of educating and enlightening. JMU has had a major impact on the city landscape and continues to exercise considerable influence on the future.

Just 180 years ago, JMU began as a small mechanics institute, established by a small group of businessmen to enlighten and educate the citizens of Liverpool for the betterment of the city. It is a mantle we have carried to this day and, although the JMU of today is a very different organisation, we continue to operate to the same driving belief that education can change the lives of individuals and bring great social and economic benefits to the city.

Much of the fabric of the city has changed thanks to the motivating force of JMU – we are not a remote campus-based university but deeply ingrained in the everyday life of Liverpool. At certain geographic points in the city centre you can see a JMU building in every direction – many of our 35 buildings act as gateways to the city centre and have become familiar architectural landmarks.

Our place as such an integral part of the city landscape has ensured that JMU is regarded locally as the obvious place to study. As universities try to encourage more people to benefit from higher education and significantly, from those communities not traditionally represented in higher education, JMU's reputation and friendly profile are regarded as less intimidating than other universities and, as a result, we have a high proportion of local students, many of whom are the first generation in their family to study for a degree.

The university has been able to transform the city landscape by encouraging young people back into the city centre, reinvigorating areas that had lain dormant for years. One of JMU's flagship redevelopments in

the 1990s was the North Western Hall, a major city building in a prime location that had been derelict for decades.

The former North Western Hotel closed its doors to the public in 1933 and for 62 years it was one of the city's most forlorn landmarks, a subject of continual public debate and a symbol of neglect. Its position, as a frontage for Lime Street and opposite the city's most famous civic building, St George's Hall, made it hard to ignore. JMU's efforts to restore and resurrect such a key building for use as a student hall of residence were rewarded by the enthusiasm of the students – few universities can offer such prime accommodation – and the resurgence in city centre living.

The economic impact of bringing student life into the heart of the city revitalised communities, bringing retail and leisure outlets into areas that had been dormant and quiet for so long. It has regenerated areas of the city centre into lively cultural centres with an energy and vitality that only younger generations can create.

The development of the Faculty of Health building and the Avril Robarts Centre in Tithebarn Street encouraged private developers to build new student accommodation in the Vauxhall area, which now thrives with the addition of over 1,000 student residents. And perhaps one of the most surprising aspects of bringing students into the area has been the integration with the local community, particularly with our international students. With hundreds of Malaysian students choosing to live in the halls of residence, we could never have anticipated that those students would be welcomed into the local bingo sessions and teach local children Bahasa Malaysian.

The integration of students into the community has been a positive force and has further encouraged local people to consider studying with us. And yet Merseyside has one of the lowest participation rates in the country for higher education:

Professor Michael Brown is the vice chancellor and chief executive of Liverpool John Moores University and took up his appointment in 2000. He started his career as a research physicist. Professor Brown is a Fellow of the Institute of Physics, a Chartered Physicist, a Fellow of the Institute of Electrical Engineers, a Chartered Engineer, a European Engineer (Eur Ing), a Fellow of the Institute of Management, a Fellow of the Chartered Institute of Marketing, and a Fellow of the Royal Society of Arts. He is a member of Liverpool First board, a member of the Merseyside Programme Monitoring committee for Objective One funding, the chair of the strategic sub-committee for Merseyside Objective One, a director of Mersey Partnership, a director of Liverpool Vision, a director of Liverpool Ventures, chairman of the Liverpool Science Park, and chairman of the Liverpool and Merseyside Theatres Trust. He is also a director of the Universities and Colleges Admissions Systems, and a member of the International Group, the Finance and Management Group, and the Leadership, Governance and Management Group of Universities UK.

the government has set a target of getting 50% of the local population into university and yet in Merseyside we currently have a figure of just 24%.

Of course, these statistics reveal a telling story, as one of the contributing factors of low participation is money. Student hardship is a very real concern to all of us in higher education and we cannot ignore the financial burden that is placed upon anyone wishing to study. At JMU we have developed a number of initiatives to help students find appropriate part-time work, and we have adapted our timetables and opening hours to provide the most flexible environment for students who also have to work.

The range of scholarships and bursaries that we can offer is increasing through imaginative schemes such as the 24/50 campaign, an initiative established to raise money to support students from Merseyside; we have a staff giving scheme to support their own students through 'give as you earn'; and we have launched a range of sports scholarships to help talented athletes fulfil their sporting potential but not at the expense of their studies.

Encouraging people into higher education will make the UK workforce much better educated and much more able to compete in the global marketplace, but our real strength in Liverpool is encouraging graduates to stay in the area. One of the major strengths of JMU is our ability to encourage enterprising graduates, many of whom go on to start their own businesses and become successful employers.

A degree at JMU is often the springboard to a different life, but more and more we are witnessing students who possess real entrepreneurial skills and talent, and we have put in place a variety of mechanisms to provide a springboard for new business ideas.

Our expertise in the digital industries led to the formation of the International Centre for Digital Content and, as this is a major growth area with so many new opportunities, we created Digital Inc to act as an incubator centre for students, graduates and, indeed, staff with new business ideas, to give them room and space to grow. New businesses need specialist help, recognising that for a germ of an idea to flourish, the right environment is required – an environment surrounded by dedicated expertise and advice

to help a business idea spin out into a new company. We even teach our undergraduates the basic techniques and mechanisms required for starting new enterprises. For our business students, a module dedicated to understanding all of the standard aspects associated with starting up a new company is built into their course, and has yielded surprising results.

During the course of a 12-week module the students must devise a dummy company, create a business plan and a marketing strategy, and approach financial advisors for backing before launching their idea. Recently, two ideas were so strong and created such a buzz that they became trading companies well before the students had graduated.

And it is not just our business students that benefit from enterprise advice: students in the arts and media are tutored on the finer points of business management, in recognition that in their chosen profession many will freelance and work independently. Recognising the reality of working life beyond graduation gives our students a remarkably solid base from which to launch their professional careers, firmly based on the practical and academic education provided by the university as one of its core missions.

JMU is an internationally recognised research university, with many of the world's finest minds working in areas such as sports science, engineering and astrophysics. These are often the headline grabbers, the ones that the media focus upon, keeping JMU and Liverpool in the spotlight. For instance, a search for JMU on the BBC news service will retrieve headlines about our sports scientists working with the international squads for the Olympics; our urban affairs specialists advising international governments on the regeneration of cities; our nutritionists working with the government on child obesity; and our astrophysicists discovering new planets and a parallel universe.

It is easy to see why such work would make the headlines, but the world-class science sitting behind those headlines is of real benefit to Liverpool. Thanks to the expertise we have developed in astrophysics, we have created a manufacturing base for making robotic telescopes and have developed telescopes for both foreign governments and private individuals. The university owns the Liverpool Telescope, which sits on a mountain in La Palma and is operated remotely from our Astrophysics Research Institute. Our telescope even features in the *Guinness Book of Records* as the world's largest robotic telescope, and it is giving schoolchildren and students unprecedented access to the night skies through the internet.

JMU's sports scientists work with international athletes and footballers to help them perfect their techniques and improve performance. Professor Tom Reilly, widely regarded as the founder of sports science in the UK, is based within our research institute for sports and exercise science and supervises research as diverse as the origins of back pain, sleep patterns, circadian rhythms and, of course, all of the aspects associated with the game of football.

And our history as a centre of excellence in maritime studies continues with new innovative precision techniques, thanks to our ship's bridge simulator at Lairdside, the only 360-degree simulator in the UK, which is used to train professional captains and pilots from all the major ports in Britain and across the world. JMU has created the opportunities for these areas of expertise to flourish and, in turn, our students are given exposure to and experience from groups of international repute. Equally, the university attracts an incredible range of guest speakers for both student and public lectures.

Our media students are particularly well served, thanks to the efforts of our professor of media studies, Phil Redmond, who has hosted a series of lectures entitled 'View from the Top', which was launched with Steven Spielberg delivering his first lecture in the UK at JMU. The series has also featured such media luminaries as Michael Grade and Greg Dyke, and the most recent lecture, presented by the former director of communications at Number 10, Alistair Campbell, who faced a daunting audience of student journalists.

JMU presents Liverpool's only public lecture series through our Foundation for Citizenship. Led by the director, Lord David Alton, who holds the May Makin Chair in Citizenship at JMU, the Foundation plays a key role in encouraging individuals to think of others and play an active role in the community. From the very beginning, the Foundation's high profile Roscoe Lecture Series caught the imagination of the local people, religious leaders, politicians, social commentators and the media, reinvigorating the debate on what it means to

The Colonnades, Albert Dock, outside the Tate.

be a citizen in the 21st century. We were particularly pleased that our most recent speaker, Nobel Peace Prize winner, the 14th Dalai Lama, took time from his official speaking engagements in Scotland to travel to Liverpool to accept an honorary fellowship from the university and share his thoughts with a rapt audience of over 2,000 people in the cathedral.

From such humble beginnings, JMU has grown to become a real force for change in the city. And it doesn't stop there. Future plans include the development of a brand new design academy, building upon the impressive heritage of our art school, whose most famous alumni, John Lennon and Stuart Sutcliffe, would surely have approved of the city's recognition as a capital of culture, and of our part in the celebrations.

A new science park for Liverpool will draw the best from all academic enterprise and give the city a hi-tech dimension; our work from the Liverpool Telescope will be given a public profile with the development of Spaceport, a new visitor attraction operated by Mersey Ferries, which will house our National Observatory for Schools, to capture the imagination of the younger generation and encourage an interest in science.

The university was praised in a government report on the relationship between higher education and business, highlighting our work in social enterprise and initiatives to support local companies, and it is an important part of our mission to interact with our communities (local, regional, national and international) and to provide the platforms for social and economic benefit. The university is proud to have played its part over the last 180 years in shaping and developing the city of Liverpool as the city achieves World Heritage site status. We intend to continue that work and to make our special contribution to the life and prosperity of Liverpool in the future.

Above all, we still hold true to our antecedents of providing opportunity for all, epitomised by our simple ethos of 'dream, plan and achieve'. We believe that, if you have a dream and the ambition and intelligence to make a plan, then Liverpool John Moores University will help you to achieve that dream.

'I blundered about happily discovering the city and its stories, being introduced to astonishing places and stumbling across myths and open secrets.'

Arabella McIntyre-Brown

see essay page 114

In Our Liverpool Home – a Heritage in Song

Peter McGovern – Songwriter of Our Times and City

The now fabled hit song *Ferry 'cross the Mersey* was barely a semi-quaver in pop star Gerry Marsden's awakening creative muse as he earned his crust as a youthful railway porter in Liverpool's Lime Street station. Meanwhile, a shuffle across the concourse, fellow railway worker Peter McGovern had already penned what was to become the first immortal anthem to the city they adored with equal passion.

Both are constantly sung – often chanted as hymns in far-off lands – by legions of expat Scousers, tears trickling down homesick cheeks as the well-loved refrains of *In My Liverpool Home,* Peter McGovern's ode, merges with Gerry's soul-filled tribute to the river and boats that give the city life.

A lyrical, big bear of a man of Irish progeny, Peter McGovern sat down to write the words in the summer of 1961 – taking two nights to wrap up the original four verses. The fledgling, soon to be world busting, Beatles were busy meanwhile 'twisting and shouting' the night away, honing their act in the seedy clubs of Hamburg's red-light quarter.

'I'd heard this old cowboy song by the Big Bill Campbell outfit before World War II called *Oh, That Strawberry Roan* with a chorus that fitted perfectly what I had in mind. So, forgive me Big Bill, I lifted that part of the tune,' confesses Peter, a huge grin spreading across his gleeful countenance.

Already then in his early 30s, Peter was a doyen of the lively folk music scene in the city that featured the likes of the esteemed Spinners and Jacqui and Bridie. His own songs and ditties, accompanied by a rhythmic guitar playing, were firm favourites. With his wife Audrey and lifelong pal Billy Moore, Peter ran the venerated Wash House folk club in Liverpool's London Road, a venue that attracted not just clutches of folkniks but unlikely pop stars such as the late Dusty Springfield. 'They'd sneak down to join us for a simple singalong after they'd wowed sell-out audiences at the nearby Empire theatre.'

Peter recalls that at one point there were 10,000 listed on the Wash House membership roll; astonishing for a club that could accommodate only 80 people, and then with a squeeze. 'Our members were flung far across the globe but kept up their links with Liverpool this way,' believes Peter.

Other memorable singers who graced the crammed, sweaty room included the grand dame of traditional folk music, Peggy Seeger, and the late Dubliner, Luke Kelly, whose soaring voice, insists Peter McGovern, is still reckoned the most powerful in the folk genre. And there was a fresh-faced if pimply Paul Simon who, on an early tour of Britain yet barely known at the time, stumbled into the Wash House one night and did an impromptu set. 'Paul actually appeared as the support act for me and Billy at a folk club in Woolton,' comments Peter convulsed with laughter, considering Paul Simon's iconic status these days. 'His next gig was in the nearby industrial town of Widnes and it was there, so it is believed, that he began writing *Homeward Bound*. I think, though, it was more probably based on the memories of being below us on the bill,' chortled Peter.

It was in the confines of the Wash House that Peter first unleashed the song that was soon on the lips of every Scouser from Timbuktu to Toronto. Today it has been embellished by over 100 additional verses, composed and sung, says Peter proudly, to mark notable events in Liverpool's contemporary history: the opening of the once luxuriant Garden Festival site, Sir Paul McCartney's knighthood and winning the European Capital of Culture crown for 2008. Now he's penned a further two verses to commemorate Liverpool as a World Heritage site. 'It would be daunting to try them all at one session but you can pick and choose the verses you want to sing to suit the mood or the occasion,' he laughed.

A few years ago Peter did organise a mammoth 60-verse singalong of *In My Liverpool Home* with another friend Spencer Leigh, the respected Mersey Beat music historian and broadcaster. They hauled in a host of celebrities and singers to the BBC Radio Merseyside studios: a motley crew that included the best selling children's author Brian Jacques, country and western singer Hank Walters, and late Mersey poet Adrian Henri.

Recorded by scores of groups and singers, oddly Peter McGovern has never made his own definitive recording of the song that is a part of Liverpool's folklore, although he has appeared on albums singing it with others and churned it out on many radio shows over the years. Now well into his 70s Peter still performs his stage act but mostly for local charities. There were times, though, when in true troubadour style he carted his trusty guitar the length and breadth of the British isles and remembers once singing that song with the Spinners at an emotional Liverpool-Everton 'derby' football cup final on Wembley's hallowed turf. 'It was great fun because we had one side of the ground roaring along to the words, and then the Everton fans booing just as enthusiastically on the other.'

Peter then laughs in his infectious rolling, rumbling manner at the memory of meeting television and show business personality Rolf Harris who told a tale of singing *In My Liverpool Home* to a gaggle of Liverpool emigrants, all living in the back of beyond in the ubiquitous Aussie entertainer's homeland. 'Rolf was astonished when they all began weeping and sighing, and it seems the song has that effect on people who move away from Liverpool,' says the loquacious Mr McGovern with a shrug of sympathy, although he winks that he's also turned tail himself and abandoned his hometown. At this he scours the horizon, leans forward and whispers conspiratorially that, although brought up in south Liverpool, he fled to Bromborough on the Wirral side of the Mersey some 20 years ago. 'Across the water ... phew ... almost a traitor, and in many ways I am an expat now.' He laughs again.

Peter McGovern is, though, even more entranced with the city of his birth than ever and gushes glowingly about its architectural heritage. 'It is marvellous that it is now finally being recognised,' he says triumphantly and then launches into one of the new verses of *In My Liverpool Home.*

In My Liverpool Home by Peter McGovern

I Was Born in Liverpool
Down by the Docks.
Me Religion Was Catholic
Occupation, Hard Knocks,
At Stealin' From Lorries
I Was Adept
And Under Old Overcoats
Each Night We Slept

Chorus
And It's In My Liverpool Home
In My Liverpool Home,
We Speak With an Accent
Exceedingly Rare,
Meet Under a Statue
Exceedingly Bare,
If You Want a Cathedral
We've Got One to Spare
In My Liverpool Home

(new verse)
Look Down William Brown Street
Your Mind Will be Blown,
By a Terrace of Buildings
Masterpieces in Stone,
Turn Round to Appreciate
St George's Hall
Architectural Treasures
That Belong to Us All ...

Chorus
And It's In My Liverpool Home
In My Liverpool Home
We Speak With an Accent
Exceedingly Rare
Meet Under a Statue
Exceedingly Bare
If You Want a Cathedral
We've Got One to Spare
In My Liverpool Home

(new verse)
They've Welcomed the World
And the World Recognised
That They're Called the Three Graces,
Our Waterfront Pride;
Three Different Styles
But so perfectly They Blend
Our Heritage, Our Home
And for Some, Journey's End ...

Chorus
And It's In My Liverpool Home
In My Liverpool Home
We Speak With an Accent
Exceedingly Rare
Meet Under a Statue
Exceedingly Bare
If You Want a Cathedral
We've Got One to Spare
In My Liverpool Home

Looking After Liverpool's Future Heritage

by Ann Lodge

In many ways our family firm is more proud of owning the Port of Liverpool building than any other in our wide portfolio, which is quite extensive and does take in quite a few other significant structures in the city, including New Zealand House in Water Street.

We took over this famous waterfront building in December 2001 – the base for many decades of the Mersey Docks & Harbour Board, and later the Mersey Docks Company – and all of us, including my two teenage sons, consider it our flagship.

When Downing was established in the mid 1980s, with our roots essentially in providing student accommodation for Liverpool's expanding university populations, we couldn't have imagined in our wildest dreams that we would eventually own one of the city's most iconic buildings: and one that is core to the city's new World Heritage status.

Of course, it is a huge responsibility and we have an obligation to look after all of the buildings for future generations. We may own them but we believe we are basically long-term curators. I was on board the *QE2* recently when she was in Liverpool and moored off the Pier Head. I stood on her deck and took a long, lingering look at the waterfront and the Port of Liverpool building.

It struck me that none of the other cities where we are now operating – Manchester, Leeds and Sheffield amongst others – can boast such a spectacular view; I thought 'you can all eat your hearts out, you don't have a waterfront like us'.

We have also set in motion an ongoing programme of refurbishment for the building and it will become a beacon once again as part of the city's lighting strategy, which focuses on illuminating a number of key buildings. It was once lit up and we are making a significant contribution to re-installing the lighting system to its former glory.

We have decided to use white light, as it will show the stonework in its natural glory. And it will also help to recreate the wonderful night-time views across the Mersey and Canning Dock.

This project is part of our ongoing commitment to regeneration in Liverpool – and increasingly other UK cities – and we were the first property developer to introduce student villages into the centre of the city, and we like to think that we helped kick-start a lot of the inner city regeneration programmes.

We actually bought and refurbished the rather dilapidated row of Grade II listed Georgian terraces on

Mount Pleasant about 15 years ago, probably the first to tackle such a project. After that we took over the former Oxford Street Maternity Hospital and the Myrtle Street Children's Hospital and – working closely with Liverpool John Moores University – we developed the site to provide student accommodation. Later we turned our attentions to the Grade II listed Eye and Ear Hospital, transforming it into a collection of desirable apartments that we have termed The Symphony; located in the heart of the city's new cultural quarter.

Our latest acquisition for the office portfolio is Federation House in Hope Street, which was, coincidentally, the base for many years of the Federation of Building Trade Employers. All these projects breathe life back into the Hope Street area.

Ann Lodge

In terms of our development projects we have a regeneration policy that aims to maintain a balance between modernisation and keeping a regard for the original heritage. This is particularly gratifying as usually it is the public sector or massive developers who handle this kind of work. We've kept it local and in the family.

And we remain an independent, privately owned firm, now the biggest property owner and commercial landlord in the city; I think we have in excess of 600,000 square feet in Liverpool alone. And we've just finished a £1 million refurbishment of No. 1 Old Hall Street, home to the Liverpool Chamber of Commerce amongst other organisations.

At one point we were the largest residential landlord in the area and we expanded into investing in commercial properties in 1997, one of the first being New Zealand House, that lovely stone building opposite India Buildings in Water Street. We also own Wellington Buildings on the Strand.

In the early stages of our investment plans we took over Victoria House on James Street, Graeme House in Derby Square – where we have just completed a £4 million refurbishment scheme – and then moved on to Old Hall Street.

We have maintained our base on Merseyside and are proud of pioneering city centre living in Liverpool. We are now introducing the same kind of expertise to such schemes as a £200 million investment to transform the former Scottish & Newcastle Brewery in Newcastle, a fine example of urban regeneration using world-class architecture, along with projects in Leicester, Manchester and Leeds.

But Liverpool was our springboard and we are delighted to have the opportunity to be involved in – perhaps even spearhead – the regeneration activities that are springing up all over the city.

We are also turning the old Hatton Garden fire station in the city centre, a Grade II Listed building, into a mix of residential apartments linked to commercial and retail space. It will provide significant new public open space as part of the overall plans.

This is an essential ingredient of all our building schemes: to ensure a sympathy with the existing surroundings, a policy we feel ties in well with the overall philosophy of World Heritage.

'... incredible, but true, that in 1848 the Liverpool Dock Trustees were better able to borrow money than was the Bank of England.'

Adrian Jarvis

see essay page 30

In some circles it is regarded as the 'existing' Fourth Grace on Liverpool's waterfront.
Constructed of opulent Portland stone and fashioned in the classic
Art Deco style this building is crested by intaglio carvings of the highest quality.
While it aspires to the exacting architectural standards of its three grander neighbours,
it is actually one of the six functional ventilation shafts for the
road and rail tunnels that snake under the river Mersey.
The striking sculpture that projects from the George's Dock side of the tower – largely
hidden from public view alongside the Port of Liverpool building –
is of the famous British aviator Amy Johnson, who made a
record-breaking solo fight to Australia in 1930.

*A ceremonial flypast of
a BEA 'Pionair Class' aircraft
(a converted Dakota) over the Albert Dock.
The aircraft flew out of Liverpool in the 1960s.*

Examples of Liverpool's architectural gems

Royal Liver Building, 1908–11, *Grade I*

Cunard Building, 1913–1916, *Grade II**

The Port of Liverpool Building, Completed 1907, *Grade II**

George's Dock Ventilation and Central Station of the Mersey Road Tunnel, 1931–34, *Grade II*

Cunard War Memorial, c.1920, *Grade II*

Monument of Edward VII, c.1911, *Grade II*

Memorial to Sir Alfred Lewis Jones, 1913, *Grade II*

Memorial to the Engine Room Heroes (of the Titanic), c.1916, *Grade II*

Other memorials at the Pier Head include:
Norwegian Seamen, *Plaque*
All Those Lost At Sea, *Stone*
Belgian Merchant Seamen, *Plaque*
Captain JF Walker CB, DSO, RN, *Statue by Tom Murphy 1998*

The Albert Dock Warehouses and Dock, Opened 1846/7, *Grade I*

Dock Traffic Office, 1846–7, *Grade I*

The Original Dock Master's Office, Albert Dock, Pier Head, 1846, *Grade II*

Canning Dock, c.1737 and 1845, *Grade II*

Pumping Station, Mann Island, 1881, *Grade II*

Salthouse Dock, c.1753, 1842 and 1853, *Grade II*

The Greater Waterfront

zone 3

Liverpool – a Potted Background

Although it is reckoned that there were some prehistoric settlers scuttling around the site of Liverpool, it was King John who established the city proper with the grant of a Charter in 1207. At that time the centre was formed from seven streets – Castle Street, Old Hall Street, Chapel Street, Water Street, Dale Street and Tithebarn Street.

The now magnificent waterfront was actually dominated for centuries by the church of St Nicholas, the Tower of Liverpool and Liverpool Castle. The city's early trade was predictably with Ireland and Scotland, but by 1550 there were also dealings with Spain, Portugal and France. By the middle of the 1600s there was increasing sea-borne traffic between the new colonies in America, carrying initially tobacco and sugar, but later cotton and, controversially the despicable slave trade, now acknowledged as a slur on human rights.

The opening of the Old Dock in 1715 further boosted the growth of Liverpool's trade and this was a key to the city's success as a port. An ongoing programme of dock construction through the 18th, 19th and 20th centuries helped continue the boom. Thus, Liverpool became the principal trans-Atlantic port of Europe for the trans-shipment of a wide variety of goods and for the soon to be mass emigrations to America, in particular from Ireland.

Towards the end of the 19th century Liverpool's docks stretched for seven miles along the east bank of the river Mersey. They were served by a commercial district of port-related offices, banks and exchanges unrivalled outside of London, and the Three Graces at the Pier Head were the city's most impressive showpiece, as they have continued to be.

The vast wealth generated by the mercantile trade was used to create a cultural quarter around William Brown Street, where the buildings and their contents remain a testament to the city's cultural values, now given a contemporary blush by this accolade of World Heritage status and the forthcoming European Capital of Culture in 2008.

The Victoria Tower – a clock bell tower of hexagon shape located in Salisbury Dock. It was nicknamed 'the dockers' timepiece'.
Folklore claims French prisoners from the Napoleonic wars built it but the dates don't tally as it was completed much later, in 1892.

'No other country
[or city] has
experienced
such a fiercely fought
competition for
the title [of European
Capital of Culture] ...'

Laura Davis
see essay page 190

How the Tide of Neglect was Turned

by Sue Carmichael

Port cites are permanently etched in my memory and have remained evocative landmarks throughout my life. Now the World Heritage site designation has awakened embedded memories of Liverpool, my adopted city, interwoven with its maritime history and its worldwide links, and juxtaposed with my more recent experiences of this great international place of connection.

Having emigrated and immigrated twice, to and from Montreal and New York as a young child, and ferried across the Mersey countless times, the city's striking skyline remains an abiding image.

Although childhood memories are inevitably ephemeral, I still have vivid recall of Liverpool; the exotically rhythmic names of the old shops we visited: Phillip Son and Nephew; Owen Owen; Rushworth and Dreaper. How I feared slipping through the gaps on the ramps to the ferries and recall being carried up a terrifyingly swaying rope ladder from our tender to emigration ship.

Apart from the dramatic and characteristic Pier Head silhouette, the most powerful memories are those that were most mysterious. I was able to work out for myself what went on behind the high fence in Birkenhead, whose enormous letters promoted Cammell Laird: to a young child the lairds 'obviously wished to ride on their camels' in private! But I was never able to solve the mystery of what happened in the gigantic brick buildings, which loomed fortress-like out of the mist as we crossed the river towards Liverpool. Their purpose remained unanswered until I returned to Liverpool a decade later.

Returning fully-grown in 1959, to what seemed a shrunken Liverpool, instantly rekindled childhood memories and heightened awareness of what I then saw as my home city. As architecture students we were required to present our first impressions through observation and sketching. Featuring the lumbering, amorphous shapes of the giant warehouses lining the waterfront, backed by countless streets of smoke-belching chimneys, my sketches captured a grimmer, starker version of the softer mood of early childhood.

Studying architecture in the 1960s fired us with a messianic zeal for the Modern Movement – the streamlined, bold and new. The past was dead and buried; we sought a brave new architecture to replace our still war damaged cities, with architectural history simply a means to an end and older buildings a mere backdrop for our visionary architectural future.

However, we were privileged to have an outstanding history and theory lecturer – the late Quentin Hughes. His unique ability was simultaneously to stimulate us to produce creative new architecture while

also cultivating an abiding appreciation of the past with Liverpool as a primary focus. Hearing about such innovative and determined young architects as Ellis, Elmes and Scott, who had respectively designed such influential buildings as Oriel Chambers, St George's Hall and the Anglican cathedral while still in their twenties was inspirational. His exciting story of Liverpool the 'cast iron shore' told of early cast iron framed churches and steel framed buildings exporting a pioneering influence across the Atlantic.

Students were required to do a measured drawing of an existing structure and Quentin Hughes, with great foresight, encouraged the study and drawing of significant Liverpool buildings. Not only did this broaden student understanding of the city's architecture, but has provided a remarkable archive of many buildings since demolished. His unique, celebratory book *Seaport* has been hugely influential in awakening wider appreciation of the city's built heritage – especially its maritime related structures. Regrettably now out of print, this great work should be recognised, together with his lifetime of passionate promotion of the city's architecture, as the very foundation of the World Heritage designation process.

Despite an external image as a city in terminal decline, its major role as a port largely redundant in a new era of air transport and European trade – the prospect of turning the overwhelming tide of neglect and negativism seemingly almost insurmountable – Liverpool still held a magnetic attraction, and we stayed on after graduation.

Also using his ingenuity to change perceptions about the potential of Liverpool, Ken Martin, then head of architecture at Liverpool Polytechnic (now Liverpool John Moores University) was celebrated for smashing china on television in a potent demonstration of the city's destruction. Leading a campaign,

Sue Carmichael currently runs the Constructive Futures consultancy with clients in the fields of architecture and cultural organisations. She was involved in writing various chapters for Liverpool's successful European Capital of Culture Bid for 2008. In 2002 her *Guide to Successful Client Relationships* was published by RIBA Enterprises and she wrote for *The Manual of Museum Planning* (HMSO, 1999). As a coordinator for Liverpool's shortlisted City of Architecture Bid she has also worked for The National Trust as Merseyside property manager, for Brock Carmichael Architects and Liverpool John Moores University. In public life, Sue is on the Learning and Skills Council: Greater Merseyside; a magistrate and deputy chair of the Youth Bench; a board member of the Liverpool Housing Trust Group; she is a Home Secretary's appointee for selecting independent members of the Merseyside Police Authority; a council member of the Merseyside Civic Society and a member of RIBA national CPD committee and RIBA/LSC client forum.

illustrated with bold sketches, he promoted moving the 'Poly', then spread citywide, to the Albert Dock, and the passion and power of his arguments won promised government funding. Regrettably the required council majority was narrowly lost and a visionary opportunity to open – finally – for public access the country's largest group of Grade I listed buildings, was squandered in a fleeting political moment.

Like many of the city's other fine Victorian buildings, the Albert Dock remained a neglected gem awaiting both a sustainable function and financial salvation. Its dock gates opened, filling the basin with a murky sludge adding to the accumulating sense of hopelessness for its future.

In the early 1980s a London based developer submitted a proposal to Liverpool city council, with a persuasive model and drawings, illustrating the necessity to fill in the dock basin to provide exhibition space. For a city in decline, such apparently seductive proposals for regeneration were always tempting.

A vociferous campaign by national and local conservation groups ensued. While any imaginative proposals for this magnificent structure were supported – it was critical that the dock basin, its very *raison d'être*, was left intact – a public inquiry lasting many weeks soon followed.

This methodical, quasi-legal process required not only thorough research and presentation by all parties, but also the forensic unpicking of the opposition's arguments. It was a huge learning curve for everyone with the collective appreciation of the significance of Jesse Hartley's internationally renowned masterpiece

Wallasey Town Hall, on the other side of the river Mersey, viewed from a boatyard on Liverpool's docksides.

becoming even more apparent, and the resulting passion and tenacity even more determined. Yet, before the outcome of the inquiry the government established the Merseyside Development Corporation (MDC) – whose area included the docks. Merseyside County Museums (now National Museums Liverpool) then achieved a longstanding ambition to expand the fledgling Maritime Museum into 'Block D' to exhibit their huge maritime collection.

Little did I realise how important my own understanding of the Albert Dock buildings could be, and the part this would eventually play in the architects' practice for which I worked gaining the Maritime Museum commission. My knowledge and unconscious affinity to the waterfront were rooted in early childhood memories which flooded back.

It is not straightforward for young architectural practices to gain large architectural commissions, as client confidence in their ability to deliver needs is acquired gradually. We were initially invited to take part on the strength of earlier historic projects where we had carried out a major rebuilding and refurbishment of a group of tiny but significant buildings: the Pier Master's House and Cooperage; and this award-winning project was remarkably challenging despite its small size.

Backed by our experience in delivering another large project, the client was confident that we had the capability for the much bigger Maritime Museum project and we were invited to join the formidable shortlist of architects. The partners won the contract by demonstrating that they had the knowledge and vision, and by displaying a sensitive response to the panel's penetrating questions.

The commission won, the practice suddenly become newsworthy; the headline in the local business news quoted the practice as saying: 'We're not whizz kids, we still wear wellies', insisting we had our feet firmly on the ground in spite of hearing that we had also won the prestigious Anglican Cathedral Precinct competition.

Delivering a project of such scale and physical and functional complexity is always a challenge. Transforming one of Jesse Hartley's warehouses – his architectural and engineering *tour de force* – into a new maritime museum

was a daunting challenge. This secure warehouse had been founded on beech piles and above ground, to be fully fire resistant, had only brick, granite or cast iron structural components, and was open fronted at dock level. Clearly new constructional elements needed to be added: windows, staircases, and a restaurant; meeting spaces as well as display areas. The developing design philosophy ensured that new interventions were distinctive while respecting and revealing, where possible, the integrity of the existing structure. The view was taken that the museum was itself an exhibit of dock architecture and conservation, and probably the only part of the Albert Dock to be retained to this degree, with commercial pressures likely to loosen the reins of stringent heritage requirements on the rest.

After much debate about options, the dockside was glazed with bold, giant sized panes of glass modulated with strong glazing bars echoing the gargantuan scale of the cast iron columns and granite dock edge. Designed in a charcoal grid pattern the carpet echoed the rough granite sets of the courtyards. Slicing through the floors, the staircase enabled the full grandeur of the building to be appreciated. In the top floor restaurant the robust but elegant tie beams are visible; colours throughout were chosen to reflect the nautical theme. New air extract ducts were freely exposed, as if on an ocean liner, and in keeping with the utilitarian nature of the original building.

Seeing this huge project take shape, together with the opening of the Tate Liverpool and the retail and residential elements of the Albert Dock, has been a huge force for change in Liverpool. Opening up these previously secure areas hitherto closed to public gaze has enabled local people and visitors to appreciate this undiscovered aspect of the city's identity and regain their connection with the waterfront and the world beyond – both literally and philosophically. Now both European Capital of Culture in 2008 and a World Heritage site, Liverpool is fast re-inventing itself on the world stage. For our maritime heritage there will be an even greater impetus to conserve, celebrate and creatively interpret not only the buildings themselves but also the economic and social background within which they were achieved. Much is made of those who made their wealth from the city and its position as a great international trading centre. We should, however, also take the opportunity to reflect on the working lives of the many construction and dockworkers who endured long hours toiling in difficult circumstances and appallingly impoverished family living conditions.

'... areas of the city centre [are now] lively cultural centres with an energy and vitality that only younger generations can create.'

Michael Brown

see essay page 52

My Liverpool:
Robin Hood was Probably a Scouser

by Professor Phil Redmond CBE

What do they say? You can take someone out of Liverpool but you'll never take the Liverpool out of them. So it is being a Scouser. Being born at the centre of the universe is something special and carries with it some onerous responsibilities, but humility is not one of them. Give a Scouser a platform and they'll perform.

The city itself is an odd place. Built on a bend in one of the world's mightiest rivers, a position well known not just for its historical context of being the gateway to the modern industrialised world, but its seven knot tidal current and that the change in height from low tide to high tide is around 10 metres. In the days of mass commuting by ferry this was what made that journey so special. Some trips you would walk downhill to the ferries waiting on the original floating landing stages. On a return trip you may have had to walk uphill.

For any mariner, whether professional or enthusiast, this is what makes it exciting, challenging and unforgiving. It is not a place for the indolent, lethargic or slothful. It is a place for the quick-witted and fleet of foot. All of which may go to the heart of what makes the city, and in turn what makes its denizens renowned the world over.

To look back at its glorious past as the second city of the world's greatest empire, the gateway to the crucible of the industrial revolution that was the North West, imbues a feeling that this was, and is, a fantastic place to be born and nurtured. A sense of history mixing with a sense of loss, together creating a sense of destiny. It is a proud as well as a burdensome mantle.

It is what confirmed the city as the European Capital of Culture for 2008. Not particularly the city's own past, present and future but the sense of creative drive that flows through its people. No matter what the arena, be it sport, arts, politics, business, science, education, health or gossip, Scousers will be in the top 10. The city has an unparalleled list of historical firsts, whether that be the first passenger railway, public health officer, steel framed building, banking computer, rock 'n' roll bands or even local politicians challenging the national system. The spirit is as alert as it is dominant.

This is what Liverpool means to me, and yet there is one other dimension. Exactly what is the definition of a Scouser? On the one hand it could simply be that once born there you are always a Scouser? Or, on the other hand, is it just enough to have been brought up or nurtured there? Then again, where exactly is 'there'?

Is it birthright or can it be given by adoption? This is an important point because while I have always considered myself a Scouser, still do and always will, under a fundamentalist interpretation, I could actually be classed as what real Scousers call a woolly-back, someone born and bred out with the sheep. I was born in the predominantly rural Lancashire. That in itself sounds a lot more genteel than saying I was born and schooled in what became two of the most socially deprived areas of the European Union: Huyton and Kirkby. However, as a child I never thought like that. Did anyone?

While the reality of Lancashire was to be a major part in that industrial crucible of the industrial revolution, from its coal mines to cotton mills, from food processing to metal working, from the age of steam to that of oil, Huyton and Kirkby were looked upon as part of the post-war rebuilding programme. They were modern garden cities. New housing developments filled with wide avenues, green parks and gardens front and rear, as well as hope for the dispossessed from the Scotland Road slum clearance programme. What we might now term social housing action programmes.

The road I grew up in, a mile or so over the city boundary, was the last in the sprawling conurbation that had the Scouse accent. At the same time I spent my secondary education some 10km further out, in Kirkby, and there the accent was alive and thick, as it was 15km further away in Skelmersdale. At no time during my formative years did I ever feel excluded from the city. Being a Scouser wasn't necessarily geographically limiting. For me the defining boundary was not physical, but audible. It was the accent itself.

That accent, like all others, derives from its historical influences. Any port, but particularly a port on the scale of Liverpool, exporting and importing people and goods from all the

Phil Redmond founded Mersey Television in 1981 and is Britain's biggest permanent employer in the independent production sector. In 1978 Phil created the BBC children's television series, *Grange Hill.* In 1982 he devised and produced through Mersey Television the pioneering drama serial *Brookside* for Channel 4 and in 1995 launched the young people's serial *Hollyoaks* for Channel 4. In 1989 he was offered the professorship and honorary chair of media studies at the Liverpool John Moores University, and later became a Fellow and Member of the board of trustees at JMU. In February 1998 he became the first chair of the university's school of media, critical and creative arts advisory board and is currently chairman of the international centre for digital content (ICDC).
Phil recently spearheaded 'Save Our Samaritans'; a media campaign aimed at safeguarding the financial future of the Samaritans on Merseyside. January 2003 marked the formation of Liverpool and Cheshire based Mersey Film. Phil was awarded a CBE for 'services to drama' in the recent Queen's Birthday Honours list.

corners of Europe and Empire, inevitably ends up as a melting pot for a wide range and diversity of tonal influences. Its guttural sound also speaks volumes for its past pollution-ridden air, but above all it is an audible reminder of its place on the world stage.

However, not all people born within the boundaries of the city have the accent. Some have deliberately eradicated it. Does speaking posh make them any less a Scouser? The honest answer is probably yes, and no. Everyone will know people, anywhere in the world, who are in denial about their birthplace or aspire to something different than the hand or accent they were dealt.

In my time as both creator and producer of popular dramas, but especially during the 21-year period when Liverpool's own soap opera, *Brookside,* graced the UK television networks, I often found myself having to defend the accent. Over the years a perception has arisen in some sections of British society that the Scouse accent is synonymous with so-called 'scally' behaviour. The likeable but roguish scallywag ready to take advantage of everyone and every situation.

To some extent there is a truth in this, traced back to the city's harsh past and transitory nature of people and trade. Employment traditions grew out of the temporary and transient nature of employment in the port and factories. With low job security, opportunism and self-preservation became the key social skills. As in any large community there will always be social misfits, but as the Scouser has been bred to play on any stage, they are therefore better able to outperform or punch above their weight than most. In any crowd you will always spot the Scouser. Therefore, the bigger the target, the easier the target, the quicker it is to label.

Like the river, the city is for the quick-witted and fleet of foot, but it is not an accent that creates the scally perception, more the acts of a minority blessed with it. We will also know many a scally with that fine-cut accent of middle England. Some of them having even been endorsed as both members of parliament and guests of Her Majesty's prison service.

Yet to misunderstand this point is also to miss a golden truth. In a harsh environment, where the skills of survival sometimes take precedence over social graces, there also develops an innate sense of natural justice. No matter what the regulations, rules and sometimes even laws say, there is a clear line about what is right and wrong. Nowhere is this more acute than in the genetically programmed Scouse justice gene. The gene which often allows the Scouser, wherever born, whatever the accent, to see and support both sides of the same argument without any contradiction.

'Working the head' is part of the game, as is accepting the 'knock-back'. If you're silly enough to allow a fiddle you deserve to get fleeced, until such time that it is deemed to be taking advantage of the less mentally fortunate. Robin Hood was probably a Scouser. Forget where they live and where they were born. It's a frame of mind being a Scouser.

It is this gene that, once again, is often misunderstood or misinterpreted as pig-headedness or even self-destructive. The dogged determination to see a cause through. A principle saved. Whether it be local politicians challenging a national government, as we witnessed during the Militant confrontation with the Conservative government of the day, or the still stoical ostracisation of a national tabloid newspaper some 15 years after the tragic events of Hillsborough. For the Scouser, if it is wrong, it can never become right.

Perhaps it is because the city is built on a bend in the river, with its back to the water. Perhaps it is because while it was once at the centre of Empire it is now on the periphery of Europe. But what is clear is that the shared sense of past and destiny has honed a clear sense of natural justice. And with it comes one more key, dynamic and special characteristic. Why answer a question when you can pose another?

Why? And, why not? These are two of the sharpest weapons in anyone's intellectual armoury. To pose the question. To test and search for the truth. Just because it is written does not necessarily mean that it is so. This sense of questioning is what makes Liverpool, and the North West of England, at which centre it sits, the most enquiring and innovative region of the United Kingdom.

So when, 30 years ago, I set out on my own particular voyage of life discovery, when I decided to abandon the relatively safe professional career world of quantity surveying, I chose a path I can now see with hindsight was driven by my Scouse genetic make-up. A path that would lead me to follow those inbred instincts of opportunism, innovation and questioning. It was the then still relatively new world of television.

In the 1970s television, despite the regional federation that was commercial television, ITV, was very much a metropolitan rather than cosmopolitan activity. More Oxbridge than red-brick. Decision making as well as most production took place in or around London and was dominated by the BBC, the state public service broadcaster. This was caused originally by technological shortcomings based on national transmitter patterns set down in the 1920s. Technology scarcity also made the BBC and ITV the only employers. London, as always, became the traditional centre. I, like many other emigrants, had to leave Liverpool and follow the route south to further my new career.

Then came the first wave of new, lightweight technology and the promise and potential of cable television, satellite services and a fourth terrestrial channel. All of which gave what every Scouser seeks: opportunity and a chance to pose those vital questions. Why? And, why not? Why can't I do that? Why shouldn't I do that?

A new market developed for independent production, programmes made outside but sold to the established broadcasters. First Channel 4 then later the BBC and ITV. Grasping the opportunity for creative control was almost as obvious as where to base a new television company. Where else but back at the centre of the universe? Where else already had such a reputation for innovation and lateral thinking? Where else was sending its writers, comedians, sportsmen and women, musicians and politicians to dominate the national and world stages? From Arthur Askey, the Beatles, Harold Wilson and Liverpool FC, the city was known for its traditional role as a pool of natural talent.

As a Scouser I knew this. There was no better place to set up a company that would attempt to do what had never been achieved anywhere else in the world. Produce two episodes of high quality drama, using untried and untested technology, as well as taking its workforce off the streets and unemployment registers. People with no formal training but enquiring minds.

In London they said I was mad. In Liverpool we know the truth. Intellectual capability is not a reflection of formal academic attainment. People rise and flourish when faced with a challenge.

The rallying cry was enthusiasm over experience, and great things are often achieved through naivety. Like scaling a mountain in a fog. You can't see how high the mountain is. It is only when reaching the summit, the fog clears and you can look back and see the height you have climbed. And so it has proved for the company I founded: Mersey Television. Now known across the world for the people and innovation it has employed, it is no longer alone. There are now many independent production companies in the UK, and some of the best are in the North West, but there is none that can rival what has been achieved at 'Mersey', on the banks of the river in Liverpool.

There is no humility, only pride in that statement. For I am a Scouser. And it is true.

It was not the buildings or history surrounding Liverpool that won its Capital of Culture title, but the people and their intellectual potential.

No one can say for certain what World Heritage status and the Capital of Culture title will bring. No one can say for certain in which direction the city will go. What form it will take. The only thing we can say for certain is that it will not be brought about by the buildings or political and social structures that form them – but only by the people that inhabit and use them. That to me is Liverpool. Not its list of fine buildings and history, but its people and their intellectual sharpness. It is on that that the future will be built.

Former warehouses in Bankhall Street.

'I had arrived in Liverpool with all the arrogance of a southerner who thought it must be grim "Up North".'

Phil Key

see essay page 176

The modern Beetham Tower majestically peeks over an old brick wall that houses the Princes Dock.

Liverpool's Different Communities
are its True Legacy

by Barbara Smith

When I left St Thomas in Barbados in 1965 Britain's immigration laws had just changed; no one could enter the country unless they had a job. Fortunately my sister was already working in Liverpool's Alfred Rose Memorial Hospital in south Liverpool and she had a chat with the matron, who kindly agreed I could take the nursing examinations.

But the Home Office was quite strict and insisted I needed the firm offer of a job before I could be granted a visa. So, using my best powers of persuasion – and in my best English grammar – I wrote to the matron again. Fine, she said, you have the job. I was just 21 and embarking on an exciting new life.

After I arrived I did take the nursing exams, of course, and actually came second in my class group; and I worked for many years as a state enrolled nurse. Later, I joined a nursing agency but had always wanted to further my education.

Naturally, I had the boys to think about – Greg, Gerry and David, my youngest at three, all born in Liverpool – but I thought it was 'now or never'; and I headed off to Hope University College to study sociology and psychology, at a time of life that many might consider quite mature.

At one point I thought the degree might open some doors for me, but there were obstacles that I didn't expect and couldn't overcome: I didn't have any practical experience in the subjects for a start and so I went into social work with Liverpool city council. I became a short-term foster carer and this has been one of the great driving forces, and passions, in my life.

In the last few years alone I've looked after five youngsters, who normally stay with me for two years or so. As a Christian I simply couldn't say no to these children. I am a committed Christian and I love being a Christian; essentially because I am a bit of a coward and it's so nice having someone you can depend on absolutely. My church is the Worldwide Church of God, which is an American-based organisation with an enormous following in Africa.

Studying was so very important to me: the whole ethos of it, the environment and the learning process. But, oddly, I was conscious that there were people I was mixing with who were never really comfortable with my colour. You see, as a black girl coming from Barbados it was difficult at times, because on the surface it all seemed very laid back in Liverpool, in England.

People would smile at you and I would take them at face value, but when I looked carefully at them, I realised that sometimes they weren't actually smiling at all, not inside. There are still times when I wonder if I have integrated. It is a good question, because I am aware of being different in this city – in this city where I have raised my family.

Despite its apparent cosmopolitan attitude there are still very few black people working in Liverpool's city centre, unlike other UK cities. It was an issue that did strike a chord with Greg, my eldest son. I was so very proud of him and his ability to cross over that racial divide. We all miss his steadying influence, but he was also irritated greatly by the divisions that exist in society, by the inequalities that allow some people to suffer.

Now, I have been in Liverpool so long that I do feel a part of it. I have seen so many changes. My first impressions as I walked down Parliament Street, a young woman from afar, was of being struck by these big, tall black buildings, all encrusted with dirt and the smoke of decades. Today the environment is so different, but I believe that more than anything this World Heritage title is an indication of a long legacy that has been shaped by so many different communities in Liverpool.

Barbara Smith

I live perfectly happily here and I don't have a desire to go anywhere else. I went back to Barbados last year for the first time in 20 years. But, after a while, it felt like it was time to come home. Liverpool is my home; I wanted to get back to my little house and my own environment. It is where I live and what I am used to, and part of my culture.

By being here, by working here, by my children being born here I am an essential ingredient of the varied culture of this great city. I never feel that I want to leave because somewhere else might be better. Barbados is a place far away that I just like to visit.

I think World Heritage and all the other recent achievements are wonderful and will bring the city to world attention again, maybe for the good things it has to offer.

I hope it will make a tremendous difference and will give people an enhanced sense of pride in our city.

So many people might now be proud to say they are from Liverpool, whereas before they might have been inclined to disguise it. I have seen a lot of things happen here in my 40 years as a citizen and I have watched my children grow. They don't really know anywhere else and this is their home. Whatever happens here affects them and me; we are a part of Liverpool's past, present and future.

Greg Greenidge, Barbara Smith's son, was born in Liverpool 43 years ago and from an early age indicated a certain promise and fascination with drama. He grew up in Toxteth and attended Arundel comprehensive school where that interest was both developed and nurtured. At 17 he was recommended for a post as a youth drama worker with the city's Community Relations Council. He based himself at Paddington school where he inspired a generation of students with his passion for drama work, devising and directing a number of thrilling theatre pieces, notably the trilogy *Street Life*.

His work at the Caribbean Centre in Liverpool influenced many other young people. He was encouraged to pursue his education further by Lady Margaret Simey, who has devoted her long life to campaigning for civil rights everywhere, not just her adopted hometown of Liverpool. And so, Greg went off to study community theatre at the famous Rose Bruford College in Kent, where he also shone.

After graduating he worked professionally in the theatre before settling into youth work – another of his interests, like photography – in Camden Town in London. He is perhaps most well known in Liverpool for appearing in several remarkable theatrical events such as *Man Friday* at the Unity theatre, produced by his former drama teacher and later close friend Peter Casey; then in Dave Marshall's lauded *Siswe Banzi;* and later in Mike Keating's production of the hard-hitting *SUS*.

He adored cricket – particularly, of course, his beloved West Indies team – and Greg's black belt skills in karate meant he had the power to kill with the bat of an eye. Yet he was the most gentle of men and, as his mother Barbara recalls, he had the ability to steady everyone he met; he was like a sturdy oak. Greg was killed in a road accident in France in April 2002, aged a mere 41; that passion and potential lost.

Now, in his memory, Greg's friends in London and Liverpool have established a charitable bursary trust,* to provide funding and support for aspiring drama students from economically deprived communities in Liverpool; young people who might see his dreams through.

* contact *www.charity-commission.gov.uk* and refer to the register for The Greg Greenidge Memorial Trust, Charity No. 1103136.

Greg Greenidge in the starring role of Man Friday, with Will Roby as Robinson Crusoe and director Peter Casey.

Paired, iron framed windows in the former Corn Warehouses at East Waterloo Dock; now transformed into luxurious residential apartments.

Examples of Liverpool's architectural gems

Princes Dock Boundary Wall and Piers. Bath Street, 1821, *Grade II*

Dock Boundary Wall from Waterloo Dock to Stanley Dock and Gate Piers, 1836–41

Waterloo Warehouse, Waterloo Road, c.1868, *Grade II*

Clarence Graving Docks, Regent Road, 1830, *Grade II*

Salisbury, Collingwood and Stanley, Nelson and Bramley-Moore Dock Retaining Walls, Regent Road, 1848, *Grade II*

Four Canal Locks between Stanley Dock and Leeds and Liverpool Canal, South of Lightbody Street, c.1848, *Grade II*

The Dock Master's Office, Salisbury Dock, 1848, *Grade II*

The Victoria Tower, 1848, *Grade II*

Warehouse on North Side of Stanley Dock, 1852–5, *Grade II**

The Stanley Dock Tobacco Warehouse, 1901, *Grade II*

Two Entrances to Stanley Dock Complex at north end from Great Howard Street and two at south end from Regent Road, c.1845–8, *Grade II*

The 'King's Pipe', Great Howard Street, *Unlisted*

The Bonded Tea Warehouse, Great Howard Street, c.1840, *Grade II*

The Business Area

zone 4

'It is a matter of having something that is exciting and daring [and contributes to Liverpool's distinctive identity] rather than safe, boring and bland.'

John Hinchliffe

see essay page 40

Tidal Barrage:
Liverpool's Influence on the World

by Arabella McIntyre-Brown

There are times when I grind my teeth in frustration at the ignorance of those who should know better. The British Broadcasting Corporation, for instance, doesn't know who invented radio. Mr Marconi, they will tell you, got there first. And there I'll be, yelling at my wireless set as though the witless presenter on Radio 4 can hear the proper answer.

Which is, as all stout Scousers will tell you, Oliver Lodge.

And when Hollywood, that bastion of All-American education, shouts the odds about George Washington and Benjamin Franklin as the heroes of the Revolution, there I'll be, shaking my fist at the screen.

For, as all stout Scousers know, they have ignored Robert Morris again. As for the futures and derivatives markets in the world's stock exchanges, those brilliant young things juggling pork bellies and Californian oranges give thanks daily to John Rew. Or maybe not. For, all too many Scousers know little of their heritage.

In a poll of the Greatest Merseysiders Ever, stout Scousers in 2003 allotted the top spot to comedian Ken Dodd. Now ... Doddy is a living legend, a star, a loyal Liverpudlian and an all-round good egg. On reflection, though, perhaps Lodge, Morris or Rew might also have been in the running. Oliver Lodge, the University of Liverpool's first professor of physics, was the first to take out patents for wireless radio and demonstrated his 'coherer' a good year before Marconi. Robert Morris, born here, became America's leading merchant and financed the American Revolution. John Rew, a Scouse cotton trader, got fed up losing money because of the long transatlantic journey and invented the financial technique of hedging.

But not one of them made it into the Top 100.

Then there are various remarkable Williams: Gladstone, Rathbone, Brown and Roscoe – politician, reformer, banker and polymath, and all of them philanthropists with chunks of the city bearing their names.

Sir Alfred Lewis Jones, shipping magnate and philanthropist, is best known for being the first to introduce bananas to Britain; John Brodie, brilliant city engineer, is best known for inventing football nets; Oliver Lodge again, better known for inventing the spark plug than for radio.

On 8 June 2004, by the way, faces around the world turned to the night sky to witness the transit of

Venus across the sun: a rare sight, first predicted and documented by the genius Jeremiah Horrox, born here in Toxteth Park in 1619 and buried there only 23 years later, having shaken up the world's astronomical community in the meanwhile. Another forgotten part of Liverpool's world heritage.

Astronomers, railway pioneers, medical pioneers, engineers, manufacturers, Nobel Laureate scientists, toymakers, chemists, artists, explorers, performers, shipowners, athletes, writers, social reformers: born in the city or attracted from the four corners of the earth, Liverpool has probably cultivated more remarkable people, per head of population, than most of the world's capitals.

Count on your fingers the cities that are recognised around the world without further qualification: and, of those, how many are not capitals?

New York, Los Angeles, Sydney, Shanghai ... and Liverpool. On my travels, if asked where I hail from, I never bother to say 'England' or 'Britain'. Liverpool is enough. And if I ask in return what Liverpool means to them, the answers include Michael Owen, the Beatles, Red Rum, ships, the war (WW2), or – curiously – suburban streets. This last from a Californian hippy chick; when I asked why, she sang a bit of the Beatles' song *Penny Lane*: '... beneath the blue suburban skies'. To Susie Blue, Liverpool was a 1960s haven of rain-soaked streets, a bit like Surbiton. When she finally got to Liverpool, in 1992, she was lost for words. And Penny Lane exceeded her expectations.

Talking of image, a city council press relations director back in the mists of time came up with the most brilliant slogan for this remarkable city. Glasgow, having won plaudits for its 'Smiles Better' come-hither line, prompted Liverpool's PR guru to dream up the immortal: 'Liverpool – it's not Surbiton'. The leader of Surbiton borough council was immediately on the news declaring in return: 'Surbiton – it's not Liverpool!'. Touché. That little

Arabella McIntyre-Brown was born and educated in West Sussex. After an idyllic summer working as a dresser at Chichester Festival Theatre with the likes of Ingrid Bergman, Penelope Keith, Tony Robinson and Oz Clarke, she went to London. There she had fun working for the Arts Council, Thames Television, assorted lawyers, English National Opera, the Transglobe Expedition – organised by her beloved late sister Ginny Fiennes and brother-in-law Sir Ranulph Fiennes – and the Royal Shakespeare Company, amongst others. She arrived in the North West of England in 1988, settled in Liverpool and became the award-winning editor of *Business North West,* followed by editorship of *entrepreneur* magazine and then as editor of *Finance North* she won the Northern Business Journalist of the Year award in 1998 and 2000. She is co-founder of *Garlic Press,* a director of *Capsicum Press* and the author of *Liverpool: The First 1,000 Years, The Grand National Quiz Book, Cross the Mersey* and the publicly lauded children's book *The Dragon That Squeaked.*

incident was at the end of what might be thought of as Liverpool's 30 Years' War. To anyone born before 1970, Liverpool's decades of decline and strife probably seem like a life sentence. Taking the longer view of the city's story, it is a blip on the graph. Since Liverpool became a port in its own right, the city has seen nearly 400 years of growth and influence, to the point in the mid 1960s when American poet Allen Ginsberg declared: 'Liverpool is at the present moment the centre of the consciousness of the human universe.'

The end of the 20th century was Liverpool's worst period since the mid 1500s, when the decayed town's shrinking population (then fewer than 1,000) had to appeal to Queen Elizabeth for help.

In the city centre today there is little reminder of the worst excesses of 1980s Militancy, let alone the grinding poverty of earlier years, when typhus and cholera wiped out thousands of those in the over-crowded, squalid courts behind the beautiful facades of the main streets. The courts have gone, but many of the beautiful buildings remain, despite the Blitz and the modernising zeal of city planners; people are coming back to live in the heart of the city.

When in 2003 Liverpool won its bid to be European Capital of Culture in 2008, I was disappointed to see how little attention was paid to Liverpool's innovative and commercial heritage; the focus was on the arts, architecture and sport. But I would argue that the culture of this city is enterprise; for centuries Liverpool has attracted entrepreneurs in all fields of endeavour, transplanted here to flourish and bloom in the rich silt of opportunity on the banks of the

The glorious vaulted ceiling spanning the arcade of shops in India Buildings in Water Street. Opened in the early 1930s as the headquarters of the Blue Funnel Line – and at a cost of £1.25 million, a staggering sum then – the structure was designed by Herbert J Rowse partly in an Italian Renaissance style.

Mersey, gateway to the world. The city is famous, these days, for pop music and football. Fair enough. The city has been very good at these things in recent decades; but there is more to Liverpool than this.

Researching into Liverpool and its millennium of recorded history for the book *Liverpool: The First 1,000 Years* I uncovered delightfully long lists of extraordinary people, bizarre stories, world-class superlatives and stunning objects. The richness of the city and its environs would give me a serious problem: how to fit it all into a single book of 240 pages, some of which would be filled with photographs? I argued with my co-author, photographer Guy Woodland, whose preference was for a book of photos with a few captions. We compromised, and I had 100,000 words to capture this city's dramatic story. It became an exercise in what to leave out: the two Liverpool favourites – football and the Beatles – had to be restricted to one page each.

Liverpudlians are quite protective of their heritage and don't like outsiders mucking about with it. When it became known in my local pub, Peter Kavanagh's, that I was writing a book on Liverpool's history, I was challenged by a character called Yusuf, a Scouser born and bred: 'How long have you lived here?'

'Thirteen years,' I replied.

'Thirteen years? Thirteen years??!!' he exclaimed. 'How can you write about Liverpool when you've only been here for 13 years?'

Quite why I feel so strongly about Liverpool and its doings is hard to explain.

Born and bred in the green lanes and orchards of West Sussex, I abandoned London after an unhappy decade there, and moved to Liverpool 15 years ago. When southern friends and family heard of this plan, they'd say 'Are you mad?' or 'Aren't you brave.'

In 1988 Liverpool was a pariah city, mired in political, economic and social quicksands, where good intentions and good ideas sank without trace unless firmly anchored to a vested interest. At least that was the consensus in all but a few tide pools of optimism. But I saw little of that. Liverpool seemed like Eden compared to London, which was huge, dirty and alien. Here, I discovered people who were open, warm, friendly, and passionate about their city. On my arrival, a tour with a brilliant Blue Badge guide called Sheila took me past St George's Hall, into the Catholic cathedral (on that sunny spring day I was drenched in the colours of the glass), down Hope Street to the Philharmonic pub and its pink marble urinals, then on to the breathtaking soaring spaces of the Anglican cathedral. I can't remember where else we went – that was it. I was sold.

The simple truth is that on the next morning, after 18 hours' acquaintance with Liverpool, I was walking across Lime Street when I realised that I had decided to move here. Like love at first sight, it happened without any conscious thought. So I went home, sold my flat and moved to Liverpool on 1st December.

I blundered about happily discovering the city and its stories, being introduced to astonishing places and stumbling across myths and open secrets. And having discovered them, it seemed bizarre that everyone in the city had not discovered them too. Let alone the world at large.

Liverpool has not, until very recently, enjoyed much positive coverage in the media. The ladies and gentlemen of the press have had it in for the city, albeit more out of laziness and ignorance than malice. When putting together a story on some burning issue of urban decay, they'd think 'Aha – I'll ring Liverpool; they're bound to have lots of this.'

And they'd send a photographer to find, or very often create, a suitably depressing image to go with their damning words. It became self-perpetuating, and getting said paragons of the press out of this infuriating habit has taken years and millions.

But at last, with the Biennial contemporary art festival in 2002, and the Capital of Culture win, the tide has changed and Liverpool has become *'Livercool'*.

So now we can shout about the city's world heritage: not just the Three Graces, the 27 million bricks of the Albert Dock, and all the marvellous evidence of our built environment, but the 1,000+ year old Allerton Oak tree, the pre-Stonehenge Calder Stones. Shipping legends like Cunard, household names like Tate, engineers like Ferranti and Laird: these were all individuals who began their businesses in Liverpool, and grew to lead the world. The driving force behind the first passenger railway was Henry Booth, a Liverpudlian engineer, an entrepreneur who brought in the great George Stephenson to build not only the locomotive *Rocket,* but also the Liverpool to Manchester railway line – which was said to be impossible. Sixty-three bridges, viaducts, cuttings, embankments, tunnel, stations and warehouses, and the line over the treacherous Chat Moss: 'perfect madness' as one critic put it.

The whole lot was built in four years.

In spite of all that, and much more, Liverpool's world heritage is as much about what the world gave to Liverpool as what Liverpool gave to the world. From the Boat People in 4000 AD, the Phoenicians, the Vikings, and on through the centuries, people of every skin colour have moored in the river Mersey to trade, to settle, to marry, to move on.

While my brothers left England to live in Canada and Thailand, and my sister ventured round the world over both Poles, I took the sensible route to the world and moved to Liverpool, where the world came to me.

Liverpool has no indigenous people – we are all incomers; it is the richness of the mix that has produced innovators, risk takers and venturers. Today the city is on an exciting upward trend, but if it is to rebuild its reputation for world-class achievement we need brave decisions and wholehearted enthusiasm. Time and tide, and all that.

Carvings depicting a grasshopper linked to a Liver Bird in Water Street. Formerly Martins Bank, this is on the next block to the Town Hall and represents the first joint-stock bank in Liverpool, in 1831. It was later acquired by Barclays.

'What strikes me forcibly about Liverpool is that it always seems to resurrect itself, and this time it feels pretty permanent.'

Steve Binns

see essay page 164

An Essential Ecumenical Synergy
for Broadening Higher Education

by Professor Gerald John Pillay

With its distinctive ecumenical tradition, Liverpool Hope University College has shared in the city's sterling efforts to improve participation rates in higher education, and to transform deprived areas that bore the worst of the aftermath of economic decline in the city's post-industrial period. Liverpool is on the rise again and Liverpool Hope proudly shares in its regeneration.

It was partly this legacy and the obvious renaissance that convinced me to accept the post of vice chancellor and move my family from the other side of the world, from New Zealand to Liverpool.

In fact, I have now discovered that the history of Hope University College's investment in the city stretches back 160 years, a truly splendid tradition of opening up access to higher education in Liverpool and throughout the North West. Indeed, Liverpool Hope's origins are in pioneering colleges established by the Church of England (1844) and the Roman Catholic sisters of Notre Dame (1856) that opened up higher education opportunities for women long before widening participation became accepted government policy.

Just over a century later (in 1964) a third college was established for both women and men. These three institutions – Warrington Training College (which became St Katharine's College), Notre Dame College and Christ's College – brought their distinct and distinguished histories into what is now Liverpool Hope University College. Today, over 7,000 students study at its two main Liverpool campuses, in Childwall and Everton, and in what is now known as the Network of Hope established in Blackburn, Bury and Wigan.

What is significant is that it is also the only fully ecumenical higher education institution in the UK. This union of Catholic and Anglican traditions with a culture of openness to all has generally proved difficult to achieve elsewhere in the UK. Liverpool's openness to different communities over a long period of time and its global outlook, being once one of Britain's main windows to the world, provided the framework for the bold ecumenical experiments that established Liverpool Hope. 'Hope' infused with rich theological meaning is also the name of the street in the centre of Liverpool that connects its two great cathedrals – a great symbol of unity.

But it is, in the end, extraordinary people willing to go beyond popular and deep-rooted conventions who break die-hard prejudices. Liverpool has been blessed with citizens like David Sheppard, its former

Anglican Bishop, and Catholic Archbishop Derek Worlock – trusted friends, pioneers and opinion makers – who became the first co-presidents of Liverpool Hope.

In modern university settings elsewhere – normally city-based and with large numbers of students – fostering student care and support, instilling collegiality and nurturing well-rounded graduates, are frequently issues difficult to achieve. Liverpool, however, is a great student city. Liverpool Hope's mission to 'educate the whole person in mind, body and spirit' is perfectly achievable here. Its educational philosophy reflects its commitment to collegiality, opening up access and service to the wider community alongside its emphasis on high quality teaching and learning, and scholarship. Hope seeks to nurture graduates who will 'make a difference'. Its goal is to remain a university with a collegial heart.

There is a synergy between Hope's and Liverpool's global vision. Liverpool's greatness in the past, when it was the second most important economic centre in Britain, depended to a large extent on its international standing. Now, once again, it is invigorated by the winning of European Capital of Culture 2008 title and was the only British nominee this year for World Heritage site status. Internationalisation is equally central to the Liverpool Hope community, enriched by the new perspectives, talents and opportunities of staff and students from over 65 countries. Liverpool Hope's international students bring home the reality that we are all members of a complex, inter-connected and ever-changing world community.

Liverpool Hope's international education charity, 'Hope One World', has grown from a single Tibetan project in India in 1981 to many cities in India (both Tibetan and Indian communities), Sri Lanka, Nigeria, South Africa, Malawi and Brazil. In this special international programme, Hope tutors and students train

Professor Gerald John Pillay is the rector and chief executive of Liverpool Hope University College, a post he has held since September 2003. Although a New Zealand citizen he was born in the former British colony of Natal in South Africa. He was awarded a BA, a BD (with distinction) and Doctor of Theology from the University of Durban and also achieved a DPhil in philosophical theology from Rhodes University. After lecturing at the University of Durban-Westville he became professor of ecclesiastical history at the University of South Africa in 1988, a post he held for eight years. During this period he was also variously guest professor at North Western University, Illinois; research fellow at Princeton University; visiting professor at Eastern Mennonite University, Virginia; guest professor at Rhodes University and visiting professor at the graduate school at AMBS, Indiana. In 1997 he became foundation professor and head of the department of theology and religious studies at Otago University, New Zealand, with promotion to head of the school of liberal arts within that university in 1998.

educators abroad in their schools and live in their villages, donating the equipment they take with them, which is paid for from funds they themselves raise. This unique global outreach was recognised in 1996 by the award of the Queen's Anniversary Prize for higher education for Hope's work with the Tibetan exile communities in Ladakh.

It is this vision to serve the world and to build bridges between community service and higher education that led to the ambitious 'regeneration' project in the Everton district of the city. By establishing a second campus in Everton, Hope turned a property with negative value into an award-winning building, which in turn helped to redeem the environment around the campus as well. The faculty of creative and performing arts located at Everton is appropriately named the deanery of arts and community.

At the forefront of regeneration in Everton, working with other organisations such as Urban Splash and the local community, Liverpool Hope has moved the regeneration frontier northwards from the city centre, attracting millions of pounds of investment and royal attention. These investments have tangibly revitalised the physical infrastructure of many economically disadvantaged communities in Liverpool, and have helped to create new gateways into higher education for those who have been traditionally excluded.

The new community-based campus in Everton is itself a reinterpretation and extension of a rich local heritage, rising as it does from the refurbishment of the derelict Grade II listed St Francis Xavier School, the former Jesuit run college that delivered up so many Liverpool people with vision and ambition. Local community partnership was achieved through collaboration with the North Liverpool Partnership, St Francis Xavier Church parish and the Liverpool Archdiocese. As with all regeneration initiatives, the project involved a cocktail of funding, including HEFCE capital funds, European Objective One, North Liverpool Social Regeneration Bid, English Heritage, Esmée Fairbairn as well as a significant capital contribution from Liverpool Hope. As a prestigious city venue, accommodating over several hundred at major events in its Great Hall, the new campus has created both work and learning opportunities for the community it directly serves.

The success of Liverpool Hope's Everton campus created a steady request from organisations and agencies for assistance in other community projects within the city. Thus Liverpool Hope's subsidiary company, Urban Hope, began specific access, regeneration and enterprise projects based on a social enterprise model to support sustainable development. This work has grown from strength to strength. Urban Hope has also developed four 'Sure Start' partnerships at Birkenhead Central and Wallasey on the Wirral, Kensington and Liverpool East. 'Sure Start' is a key government initiative targeted at the poorer wards in England and involves a multi-agency approach to providing support for families with young children. Education and widening access are thus inextricably connected.

Urban Hope has also been commissioned by four partnerships to develop their capital strategies – two of these Liverpool-based programmes in Kensington and Liverpool East are now at an advanced stage. In Kensington, the construction of a £3.6 million family and lifelong learning centre will provide a quality physical base for education, health and social service agencies to work together under the umbrella of a children centre status. In Liverpool East, a family, training and health centre to house 'Sure Start' and a community health provision will be completed in 2005.

All of these projects live out the mission of Hope. They involve partnership, offer quality support and expertise to enable reinvestment in deprived communities, and create tangible opportunities for education and social well-being. These projects recognise the importance of a higher education institution taking an active role in the regeneration process to reclaim a proud city heritage.

Working in partnership with the key business support agencies, Liverpool Hope also plays an increasingly significant role in the economic regeneration of the city and region through the provision of business improvement programmes and the training and development of the workforce. The unique graduates for Merseyside initiative has helped to increase graduate retention levels, ensuring that the city continues to benefit from a substantial base of highly skilled young people.

The unique features of Liverpool's people, their challenges and their hopes, has helped to shape the story of Liverpool Hope University College. Its academic and scholarly goals are tied to key commitments arising out of its unique ecumenical foundation and its mission: moving education out of the ivory tower, giving the excluded opportunities that class and elitism deny them, educating in the round, nurturing a supportive scholarly community and providing graduates with a keen sense of purpose in a changing global society. Research and high quality teaching are paramount at Liverpool Hope University College; but so is the will to create a humane and enlightened society.

Even the Turbulent Irish Sea is no Barrier to the Lure of Liverpool

It's a fair old hike from the rolling fields of Mayo in the west of Ireland, to the windy, concrete canyons of Chicago, or from the quiet countryside of Newtonards at the head of Strangford Loch in Northern Ireland to the Strand in Liverpool; but the city's net is hurled far and wide.

Maggie O'Carroll grew up near the small town of Ballinrobe in Ireland's far west at a time when the Celtic Tiger was yet to whimper never mind roar. She headed off on that traditional Irish route to America seeking opportunities and the chance to shine. Chicago kept her in its grip for several years but a casual trip to Liverpool to visit friends changed her life, maybe forever.

Meanwhile, Lisa McMullan had left the family home in County Down and set off for Liverpool's then polytechnic to tackle a business degree; got it and quickly shifted out to London eager to make her mark.

She admits that when first clapping eyes on Liverpool there were fleeting moments of doubt; the city, recalls Lisa, was very bleak and grey. 'But I was a student and didn't have much money. And I thought this was what I should do: sit and drink in sad old pubs and dirty places. It was all part of my learning experiences.'

But the peculiar lure of Liverpool drew her back. She became a women's economic development officer with Liverpool city council and set about trying to redress the imbalance in the business sector that almost denied women the breaks and support that could help them break the shackles of unemployment; maybe even go into business on their own, an unusual occurrence in Liverpool especially a decade ago.

Later, she joined the trail-blazing women's training and advisory organisation Train 2000 whose activities in the last eight years have earned accolades from such luminaries as Patricia Hewitt, the British government's trade and industry minister and

Maggie O'Carroll

Lisa McMullan

Cherie Blair, the wife of the Prime Minister, who was herself raised in the Crosby area of the city.

Lisa reveals that they've been consulted by almost 2,000 women in the last two years, and helped more than 200 in business start-ups. 'The city is surely different from when I first arrived, almost totally transformed and feels more upbeat. Mind you, I am conscious that in some of the minority communities and outlying districts there are still problems. But I'm delighted that the city seems to be on an upward swing and I'm staying put as one of the new settlers who's been won over.'

It was the same for Margaret O'Carroll who found Liverpool almost a depressingly down-at-heel reflection of her homeland when she first took a ferry across the Mersey. Ireland was on the verge of an economic and social metamorphosis and Maggie reckoned there was a similar spark in Liverpool about to ignite.

With a business degree under her belt she became a consultant but soon realised that it was the social enterprise sector in the city that could really benefit from her skills. With a couple of colleagues she set up Train 2000 and has since been the driving force behind the establishment of the Merseyside Social Enterprise Initiative, which has brought together a partnership that includes the North West Development Agency, the EU Objective One programme and Greater Merseyside Enterprise amongst others; pumping in a £20 million investment package for aspiring social enterprises across Liverpool and the region in general.

Having completed further studies at Cambridge University – a masters in community enterprise, the first of its kind in the UK, and for that matter internationally – and with her background in helping develop the strategic framework for women's enterprise, a ground-breaking initiative that has high level UK government and EU Brussels backing, and commitment to a number of influential nationwide and European organisations, the world beckons.

But it can wait, as Maggie confesses that she became enmeshed in Liverpool from the moment she set foot in the city. 'There is a remarkable buzz about the place that was lacking before, but there is a significant amount of work to be done in terms of women's entrepreneurship, and the issues of social and economic inclusion within deprived communities,' she comments.

'Things are getting better but we need to refocus our efforts to establish a fully inclusive city, where all its citizens can enjoy these terrific achievements such as Capital of Culture and World Heritage status. I live in Toxteth, which is a grand area and I intend to stay; the city has me in its thrall.'

'... there is ... a certain irony that [Liverpool's] success as a trading city depended ... on its ability and willingness to innovate ...'

Drummond Bone

see essay page 154

Liverpool – Now Stretching Beyond its Imperial Past

by Ian Wray

Liverpool is not a provincial city; it is an imperial city. Only by accepting this proposition can one begin to understand its uniqueness, its cultural history and its architectural inheritance. Historian Jack Simmons had an instinctive feel for it: 'Liverpool has a quality to be found in the same abundance nowhere else in England: the quality of grandeur.'

The quality appears abroad, of course, though less commonly than you might think. Liverpool, said Simmons, has it endlessly, in its site on the broad Mersey estuary, in the terraced city rising above it, in its topography, its great buildings and its monuments to civic pride. In almost every sense Liverpool is a European city, a city which for good or bad has helped to shape world and European culture.

Journalist Graham Turner visited in the 60s, a time when the city was brimful of post-war confidence. Liverpool, he claimed, was typical only of itself, and for that reason alone could not invite indifference. 'The most important result of the city's constantly changing population' said Turner 'is that nothing is fixed, that everything is in a perpetual state of flux ... so Liverpool is a city in which there are no preset responses; everything is played off the cuff. The place is full of strange sights and sounds. Two men carrying suitcases stagger up the hill from the Pier Head to Jack Montgomery's Antrim Hotel. The names of the streets and factories are extrovert, ambitious: Venus Street, Apollo Street, the Odyssey Works. Another 60s' visitor, the architectural writer, Ian Nairn, evoked a similar response: 'The scale and resilience of the buildings and people is amazing – it is a world city, far more so than London or Manchester. It doesn't feel like anywhere in Lancashire: comparisons always end up overseas.'

Although chartered as a town in 1207, Liverpool did not become a place of any size until the middle of the 18th century. It rose fast in the 19th century as Britain's greatest imperial seaport. From the outset its trade related to the colonies and the empire, which even by the 18th century had eclipsed all its rivals.

Did the British Empire benefit its subjects? In some ways perhaps it did. Certainly the British thought they were on a civilising mission. Yet no one can dispute the despicable cruelty of the slave trade, in which Liverpool merchants played a leading role. It remains a sensitive issue that cannot be overlooked.

As the World Heritage nomination acknowledges, the slave trade played its part in Liverpool's 'stupendous development'. Slaves were not shipped from Liverpool itself. They were taken on board in

west Africa where outward bound cargos were unloaded, and endured the horrors of the 'middle passage' across the Atlantic before ships returned to Liverpool with raw materials from the Americas. It was said to be an 'amazingly lucrative' triangular traffic by which 'a treble profit was made on every voyage'. For the Liverpool merchants, the slave trade brought riches. For the slaves it brought misery.

Generations later came another consequence of that trade, black Americans became an unexpectedly powerful and creative voice in 20th century world culture. In cities like St Louis, Memphis and Chicago African musical culture mingled with European musical instruments and forms. The outcome was black American music – blues, soul, gospel, rhythm and blues and jazz – the latter arguably the most wholly original and creative 20th century art form.

By a strange twist of history the emergence of black music renewed Liverpool's American connections, and its role on a world stage. Through the 1940s and 1950s records by American blues, R 'n' B and soul artists arrived on American liners and freighters. A new generation of young white musicians began to listen to the black originals, as well as white American artists like Elvis Presley, who were fusing the blues with country music to create rock 'n' roll. Liverpool was to British rock as Memphis was to American. There are many reasons: the port, the American trade, the cultural and racial mix, the flux, the dislike of conventions (noticed by Graham Turner).

John Lennon, Cilla Black, Gerry Marsden (alongside many forgotten names like Rory Storm, and the Big Three) took the elements of both black and white popular American music. They created an original Liverpool sound which was amplified, refined and re-transmitted to white America. Lennon is reported to have said: 'It was black music we all dug – we all listened to

Ian Wray is chief planner at the North West Development Agency. Prior to this he had 20 years' experience of planning and regeneration projects in North West England, particularly in Merseyside and in Liverpool's inner city. He coordinated 'Greener Growth', the North West's regional planning advice, in 1994. Born in Manchester, he was educated at the University of Newcastle upon Tyne and University College London. He now lives in Birkenhead with his wife and two teenage daughters.

Sleepy John Estes. We can sing more coloured than the Africans.' Richard Florida, professor of regional development at Carnegie Mellon University, is the new American urban thinker. Florida has introduced a theory of city development, which centres on the rise of a 'creative class'. Creative people, says Florida, do not simply cluster where the jobs are. They seek out places which are centres for creativity and where they want to live. They like city regions which offer economic opportunities, a stimulating environment (including a restored heritage) and all the amenities for active outdoor recreation. Florida's research has tried to uncover the underlying conditions that enable some places to attract and retain their creative classes more than others. He finds that tolerance and openness are critical. Places where gays, immigrants and bohemians all feel at home and where different racial groups live together are very likely to have this attractive culture of tolerance.

Florida is good at analysis, less good at prescribing cures. He is sure that the presence of a university is important, acting as a creative hub: many of the most creative cities in the US are also home to major universities. He knows that the creative class likes to live in restored old properties and historic quarters, and that they value access to the outdoors life. Beyond that Florida is struggling. And perhaps there is a good reason for that. It may just be that creative places cannot be artificially created. Maybe they just have to emerge organically, through a series of happy accidents. Oddly enough a 'creative class' started to rediscover Liverpool city centre sometime in the early 1990s – before Professor Florida had written his book.

The process was kick started by the former Merseyside Development Corporation, who saw residential apartments as an important component in their plans for bringing the Albert Dock and Wapping warehouses back to life. Yet there are deeper

causes. Liverpool's inheritance from the past includes many of Richard Florida's conditions for success: bohemian culture, two university 'creative hubs', and an architectural heritage and townscape which is second to none. It is a very good place to live.

Here a happy accident played its part. Ambitious plans were laid for the city centre in the 1960s. 'Widespread obsolescence – about two-thirds of the city centre is in need of renewal ... presents redevelopment opportunities unequalled by any other major city in this country.' So wrote the enthusiastic authors of the 1965 'City Centre Plan'. But the plan's ambitions came to earth with a bump. Through much of the following 30 years the city's economy went into reverse. The plan was never carried through. Large swathes of the 19th century city centre remained intact, waiting for new uses.

The growing residential market is one of these new uses. Between 1991 and 1999 the city centre population grew by almost 300%, from 2,340 to 9,000. Today investment is led by private developers, often small scale. Much of the urban design is arresting and imaginative. A building like the derelict former Plessey factory in Cheapside seemed fit only for demolition in the early 1990s. Now, like many others, it is a strikingly attractive housing development.

The city planners made their own contribution to the process, by vacating their dreary office block on the Strand. Ten years on, thanks to an inspired refurbishment by developers Beetham and architects Brock Carmichael Associates, it is Beetham Plaza. New city dwellers kick back in chic apartments, where once the planners hatched their schemes.

Who are these new city dwellers? To answer the question the late Professor Moss Madden, Vicki Popplewell and I collaborated on a survey of new residents in 1999. The results showed that the new properties were catering for a significant new market. The residents were overwhelmingly male, single and slanted heavily toward the managerial and professional classes. There was a clear bias towards the 21–40 age group: they made up 59% of the new city centre population. Amongst long stay residents 69% had a university degree, whilst 49% had a postgraduate qualification. A new high status housing market is being created from scratch, and the process very visibly continues today.

City of Culture, City of World Heritage, City of the Creative Classes – has Liverpool discovered a new strength, or rather rediscovered some old ones? Certainly there is a new mood about, not unlike the high confidence of the 1960s. And this time the process seems more deeply rooted.

But predictions are a risky business. Perhaps it is better to leave the final words to Daniel Defoe, whose travels brought him to Liverpool in 1708: 'Liverpool is one of the wonders of Britain ... a large, handsome, well built and thriving town. It still visibly increases both in wealth, people, business and building: what it may grow to in time I know not.'

Examples of Liverpool's architectural gems

Liverpool Town Hall, Castle Street, 1749–54; 1789–92; 1795–1820, *Grade I*

Bank of England, Castle Street, 1845–48, *Grade I*

Adelphi Bank, Castle Street, 1890–92, *Grade II**

Monument to Queen Victoria, Derby Square, 1902–06, *Grade II*

Nelson Memorial, Exchange Flags, 1813, *Grade II**

Tower Buildings, Water Street, 1908, *Grade II**

Oriel Chambers, Water Street, 1864, *Grade I*

India Buildings, Water Street, 1924–31, *Grade II*

Barclays Bank (formerly Martins Bank), Water Street, 1927–32, *Grade II**

White Star Building (Albion House), James Street, 1898, *Grade II**

Rigby's Buildings, c.1850, *Grade II*

Royal Insurance Building, Dale Street, 1897–1903, *Grade II**

The Temple, Dale Street, 1864–65, *Grade II*

Municipal Annexe, Dale Street, 1882–83, *Grade II*

City Magistrates' Court, Dale Street, 1857–59, *Grade II*

The Albany Building, Old Hall Street, 1856, *Grade II**

Cotton Exchange, Old Hall Street, 1906, *Grade II*

Hargreaves Building, Chapel Street, 1859, *Grade II*

The Cultural Quarter

zone 5

'On board the *QE2* ...
I took a long, lingering
look at [Liverpool's]
waterfront and thought
"eat your hearts out"
[everywhere else] ...'

Ann Lodge
see essay page 68

Now the Fog has Lifted –
Liverpool Looks to the Future

by Joe Riley

There is a four-letter word which ideally sums up Liverpool's changing image in the 40 years separating the Beatles from World Heritage and Capital of Culture status. And that word is soot. I should know. My great-grandfather founded a coal merchants at Bank Hall which only closed down in the wake of the new smokeless zones introduced during the mid 60s.

Prior to that, from the time the first Cunard liners billowed murky plumes into the salt-sea air, and the first steam engine shunted into Lime Street, the fine buildings we salute today were steadily being covered in an acrid tar common to all great cities of the post-industrial revolution. Even up to a decade ago, many then living into their late 80s had quite forgotten that St George's Hall, the noble facade of William Brown Street and the Three Graces of the early 20th century, had all at one time boasted clean faces.

And apart from soot, there was another main contributory factor. Fog. No, more than fog. There were the peasoupers that would last four or five days. Fogs so bad that pedestrians walked spectre-like in front of vehicles carrying yellow-hued torches. Fog not only formed outside buildings, but also inside.

During the 1980s, when I was one of the few privileged to go into St George's Hall to play the great 7,000-pipe Willis organ – to save it from rotting away due to no heating and drenching humidity – a pall of fog would form around the granite pillars and up to the vaulted ceiling. As I glanced in the music desk mirror at the console, I would not have been surprised to see the ghost of gallows-bound poisoner Mrs Maybrick through the open portals of the deserted courtroom at the other end of the hall. The crown courts had long departed St George's Hall for a modern home in Derby Square. As the Home Office had paid 90% of the running costs for what was Queen Victoria's favourite public building, the hall, neglected by the city council, faced ruination.

Liverpool, in the grip of Militant Tendency, had little time for spending on heritage – just as an earlier Labour administration, in common with its counterparts throughout the UK, had bulldozed Georgian, Victorian and Edwardian elegance in favour of building egalitarian concrete citadels like St John's Market, Concourse House on Lime Street, and some other still surviving monstrosities. Under Militant, St George's Hall would have been mothballed and left to rot. Fear of a similarly bereft future for Liverpool's museums and art galleries led to them being financed directly by Whitehall instead of being left to the whim of indifferent local government. But Militant itself passed into the looking glass of history. And with them went the fog of political ineptitude, and finally the physical fog which had cloaked the city's skyline.

Sporadically from the mid 70s, government schemes began to underpin the cleaning of buildings. That improvement has ever gathered momentum, until the most recent £15 million makeover for St George's Hall, due for completion in April 2005. Today, Liverpool is in the midst of a £1 billion refurbishment and expansion; a city once more on the brink of self-fulfilment. Despite the grime, Liverpool, even at the height of its last wave of economic good fortune, had been a commercial rather than an industrial centre: a place of shipping, insurance and banking. Each of these interests owned a building and wanted to promote it. There was tremendous rivalry, and a great deal of experimentation and innovation.

As for trend-setting, it was the late historian Professor Quentin Hughes who pointed out to me that the first 'modern building' in the world was St George's church on Everton Brow: the primary example of prefabricated, factory-constructed large-scale pieces, made in advance, brought to a site and then bolted together. The year was 1812, almost 40 years before the Great Exhibition and the building of Crystal Palace. But the architect of Crystal Palace knew Liverpool – just as French emperor Napoleon III was once exiled to Southport. His commission for the redesigning of Paris with its wide boulevards was, mused Professor Hughes, based on Lord Street in the seaside town. If I digress by appearing to be 20 miles north of target, there was a connection.

The new and magic ingredient for all this activity – in Liverpool and elsewhere – was iron. Liverpool has the oldest example of part of a building held up by iron columns. That is

Joe Riley was the youngest arts editor of a major British newspaper when appointed to the *Liverpool Echo* in 1974. Thirty years later, he is the longest serving journalist in such a post. His work has taken him all over the world, including more than 25 foreign tours with the Royal Liverpool Philharmonic Orchestra. As the *Echo's* award-winning film, theatre, music and fine arts critic, Joe has interviewed the leading names in the arts and show business, as well as all of today's top Hollywood stars. He is a regular broadcaster, festival adjudicator and master of ceremonies at major events, including the Liverpool Summer Pops which attracts and presents stars of the calibre of Sir Elton John, Bob Dylan and Jools Holland. In July 2002 Joe was honoured with a fellowship from Liverpool John Moores University for his 'outstanding services to the arts on Merseyside', thereby joining the exclusive ranks of the JMU's other media alumni, Sir Andreas Whitham-Smith, Sir Trevor McDonald and his own former *Liverpool Echo* colleague, the now internationally acclaimed television celebrity, Anne Robinson.

St James's Church, Upper Parliament Street, dating from 1774. This use of iron became the basis, through steel, of virtually all 20th century construction. Indeed Tower Building, near the Pier Head, was the first steel-framed building in the world, while the facing Royal Liver Building – by the same architect – was the first multi-storey concrete building.

Even more remarkable, some would argue, was the work of 1930s' Liverpool city engineer, Alexander Brodie, who designed the prototype for prefabricated reinforced concrete buildings. These had their doors, windows and other features cast into the structure in the factory and became the basic form of all high-rise building. One scarcely needs to spell out the impact of such endeavour. The whole of the Soviet Union, China, America and France adopted the Liverpool engineer's principle.

Whatever people's feelings today about high-rises – and many such flats in the city have now come down – the ultimate irony was that during the 60s Liverpool had to commission a French firm to do a copy of Brodie's original idea.

What has happened in more recent years is still being assessed. Thank God that so many of the great swathes of Georgian and Victorian housing surrounding Liverpool's plenteous parkland was preserved at the eleventh hour from neo-socialist idealism. The suburbs of Liverpool were never destined to become the outskirts of Moscow.

Equally, the late 90s redevelopment of Queen Square, a huddle of buildings cheek by jowl with poor use of intermediary space, and divided by a bus lane full

The base of the Wellington Memorial at the east end of William Brown Street.
Erected in 1863 it is a monumental public sculpture of 40 metres in height,
and the 'Iron Duke stands atop a fluted Doric column.
Depicted is part of the frieze detailing his battles.

of half-empty vehicles belching exhaust fumes, is an undoubted folly. Do we really want to return to those grime-encrusted buildings? I think not, particularly as plans are afoot to stop even human beings from smoking. Traffic control, adequate parking facilities and an increased emphasis on pedestrianisation are all things for consideration in the run-up to 2008.

As I recall sitting on my father's shoulders, high above the crowd, to see the last tram depart the Pier Head in 1957, it seems significant that nearly half a century later we are awaiting the first part of a new tram system costing more than £650 million. They say bring back the overhead railway. They say build a third Mersey Tunnel. They say let's have another Mersey bridge crossing between Widnes and Runcorn. There's a difference between conjecture and what can reasonably be delivered.

Liverpool is currently being refurbished 'floor to ceiling.' Granite sets, like the ones that lined the cobbled streets in granny's day are being re-laid. Above, scaffolding rising in some cases hundreds of metres into the air, recasts the crowns and coronets of an earlier architectural age.

As was so notably pointed out in Liverpool's European Capital of Culture submission, the city's architecture 'forms the stage on which we live out our lives.' In that sense, it is the most basic art, from which the enjoyment and appreciation of all other art flows. Whether that be ideal acoustics at the Philharmonic Hall, a fine refurbishment of former warehouses to form a home for Tate Liverpool, the Maritime Museum and the Museum of Liverpool Life; the expansion of the Empire theatre or a new interactive website at the museums or at the Foundation for Art and Creative Technology (FACT), comfort is now an integral part of how we assess the quality of life and value for money. The £10 million refurbishment of the Philharmonic Hall during the late '80s led the renaissance of these more aesthetic values. The Walker gallery, the main city museum, the Tate, and even tiny and artistically ground-breaking Unity theatre followed suit.

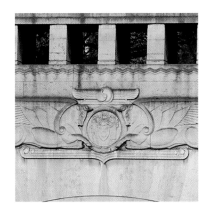

Even the Royal Court theatre, wholly dependent on private money, was given a new coat of paint inside and out. No matter how much sentiment people felt (and still do feel) for the old Everyman, Playhouse and Neptune

theatres, they are clearly not going to serve the city and region's needs into even the near future. A new 'theatreland' has been suggested adjacent to Williamson Square. Time will tell.

A 9,000-seater stadium is planned for Kings Dock. The Fourth Grace – architect Will Alsop's controversial Cloud – could provide a second home for museum artefacts. Incidentally, the Fourth Grace is likely to be no less or more an issue of debate than the passing outcry which greeted the completion of Liverpool's Metropolitan Cathedral in 1967. It has always been thus. Look at the derision Parisians heaped on the Eiffel Tower, designed to last a year, and still standing more than a century later.

Prince Charles' well-known reservations about modern design proved a wet blanket to British initiative, which readily explains why most of the best work by British architects is now done abroad. But as handsome Liverpool regains its more youthful looks, the single thing which marks out our role as a city of world-class heritage has to be the audacity shown by our forebears.

Who had the foresight (even though it never came to full fruition) to approve plans for a Roman Catholic cathedral even bigger than St Peter's in Rome? The citizens of Liverpool did. Likewise, who had the temerity to suggest (and complete) the building of the largest Anglican cathedral in the world? The citizens of Liverpool did. Both these grand ecclesiastical undertakings furthered the proven glory of a civic hall (opened 1854) which has been hailed by the *Architects' Journal* as the greatest revival of classical architecture mankind has ever witnessed. Not only all this, but also the taking of risks. The architects of the Anglican Cathedral and St George's Hall, Giles Gilbert Scott and Harvey Lonsdale Elmes, were respectively aged 21 and 24 when they won the design competitions.

It is, of course, a source of wry amusement that Liverpool can be proposed as, and succeed at becoming, a World Heritage site without the inclusion of the cathedral. There is simply so much of worth, that Scott's great sandstone edifice does not need to be a component part of that winning argument. Astounding, especially in a city which is less than two miles in diameter and which, it could be argued, has only three main east-west thoroughfares and two running north to south.

Contained within this compact 'village' are some of the greatest gems of building achievement to be found anywhere. It is a valiant claim which can be justifiably made despite a history incorporating famine, epidemic and blitz.

If I had been but 10 years older, it would have been my fate (and probably considerable fortune) to have covered, as a journalist, the rise of the Beatles. On a less salutary note, I did cover the in-filling of the original Cavern club, which must make some bureaucratic hearts miss a beat among the annals of retired town hall officials. But I can be equally proud to have covered the story of a city in renaissance. A place which once again believed that the mantle of the merchant princes of Florence had fallen upon its shoulders, and which can clothe itself afresh in the garments of prosperity.

Had I been standing with pen and notebook in Mathew Street in 1961, I would not be covering the monumental events leading up to the city's 700th birthday in 2007, and of Capital of Culture a year later. I am more than content that my era of Merseyside-based artistic enlightenment included such luminaries as Simon Rattle, Margaret Simey, John Moores, Clive Barker, Julie Walters, Peter Postlethwaite, George Costigan, Jonathan Pryce, Barbara Dickson, all the bands at Eric's, Willy Russell, Alan Bleasdale, Jimmy McGovern, Adrian Henri and Arthur Dooley. The list could go on ... and on ... but one name covers the entire period: Ken Dodd, the last in a long line of great music hall stars, and voted Greatest Ever Merseysider in a *Liverpool Echo* poll. Alas, we have not preserved the jam butty mines of Knotty Ash. But they have made a visitor attraction out of the miles of tunnels burrowed under the city by Joseph Williamson, the so-called Mole of Edge Hill.

Overground, underground, at street level and high in the sky, Liverpool has relearned how skill and determination have turned up trumps once more. The one-time Second City of the British Empire is now the epitome of the 'world in one city', as well as the First City of European Culture and British cultural heritage.

Lime Street station next to the imposing grandeur of the former North Western Hotel, which boasts a monumental façade in French Renaissance style.

'... we arrived by bus
in Liverpool,
and it was the first time
in my whole life
that my family and I
felt free.'

Saranda Hajdari

see essay page 196

Universities Set Cultural Values
but are Equally Economic Drivers

by Professor Drummond Bone

The University of Liverpool has recently celebrated 100 years of its Charter, though its origins go back much further, to the Medical Institute founded in 1834, as a response to an outbreak of cholera in the city two years earlier. The university's life therefore spans the range of Liverpool's existence, from a global city in the Victorian period through the troubles of the years following World War II and on into its current rebirth. It is for its trading and industrial past that Liverpool has come to achieve this World Heritage status, and there is in this a certain irony that its success as a trading city depended precisely on its ability and willingness to innovate, sometimes at the expense of the past. In many ways universities are a microcosm of this paradox.

The great civic universities of 19th century England, and Liverpool is no exception, were set up by their city fathers partly, certainly, out of an impulse to lay down for posterity their own cultural values, but at least as much as (in modern terminology) the economic drivers of their city. Guardians of civilisation, the universities were also, as they are once again, the generators of innovative ideas and the generators of wealth. That the great dockland areas of Liverpool are now again producing wealth, though not in the way originally intended to be sure, gives this dual notion of their particular heritage a unique potency.

This ever unstable dynamic of transient but ever renewing innovation on the one hand, and the will to permanent values on the other, is not only then a mark of the city (with its Roman motto and monumental Three Graces dedicated to those on the move, those on the move moreover often with no very clear idea of their destination), but also of the city's university specifically. The university's current management school, for example, is housed in a complex having its origins in 1860 as a Welsh Calvinistic Methodist chapel. This Italianate building of brick and painted stone by Oliver Mann, which owes its existence to the rising immigrant population from Wales, has now moved from a commitment to the other world to a celebration of entrepreneurship.

The Victoria Building, one of the great city landmarks, and at least arguably the origin of the tag 'red brick' for the 19th century civic universities, has on the other hand yet to find a new role. Originally built by the eminent architect Alfred Waterhouse, who through his love of bright red brick gained the unkind if not entirely inappropriate sobriquet of Slaughterhouse Waterhouse, this building was intended for entirely practical purposes, and originally housed the offices of the principal, registrar and administrators of the university. Moreover it was surprisingly high tech, including fire-proofing offered by an iron sub-frame and concrete floors, as well as extensive use of steel in the clock-tower, electric lights and lightning conductors. But like the wonderful tobacco warehouse on the Stanley Dock, its very practicality for a specific purpose has rendered it difficult to adapt to a new age. In neither case however is hope lost, and in both cases the practical may be reborn for cultural purposes.

The university offices are now housed in a building dating from 1966, inserted into the side of Abercromby Square which itself was a centrepiece for housing development laid out from 1820 onwards and including, at No. 19, a building with splendid painted ceilings once used as an unofficial Confederate Embassy during the American Civil War. Just how successful from an architectural point of view this insertion of the 60s into the early 19th century is can be debated, but the point once again is that the university represents not only preservation of the cultural heritage but also its innovative renewal. Modern industry inside the university is represented by the Life Sciences Building completed in 2003, lying at the north-east corner of the university, in which takes place not only fundamental science but also the commercialisation of that science in the service of what we might now call the health industry.

This takes us back full circle to the Royal Infirmary, and the reason for the establishment of the university. The chapel of the Infirmary is now incorporated into the university's research and business service activity, providing a dramatic example of the re-birth of a building dedicated to eternity as a lively and successful centre for commercial activity. It is this wonderful and ever changing incorporation of industry into heritage and heritage into industry, a mark of the city and original university.

Professor James Drummond Bone MA, FRSA has been vice chancellor of the University of Liverpool since September 2002 having previously been principal of Royal Holloway, University of London. He was also dean of the faculty of arts at the University of Glasgow, his own *alma mater,* from 1991 to 1995 and vice principal until 1999.
Professor Bone takes a particular interest in the links between higher education and both the private and public sectors as reflected in his membership of the European Union Programme Evaluation Panel for the West of Scotland, the Scottish Council for Development in Industry and the Board of the Scottish Biomedical Research Trust and the Strathclyde European Partnership. He is a consultant on higher education financial management to various organisations including the Argentine ministry of education; a board member of the Surrey Economic Partnership, and an advisor to the South East of England Sustainable Development Group. He is on the board of trustees for National Museums Liverpool and the Liverpool Capital of Culture board.

One of the grandest and most elegant 'classical' buildings in Europe,
St George's Hall – built between 1840 and 1855 –
boasts a 'free' neo-Grecian exterior, which encloses a
richly adorned Roman-style interior.

Homesickness

by Peter Grant

Mum was always ironing. Even when I came running home in the rain one day clutching a copy of my first ever record – *Sgt Pepper's Lonely Hearts Club Band.* Mum just nodded when I told her I'd spent all my pocket money on it. ... all £2. She ironed my school uniform as if putting the finishing touches to a painting.

Home is where the heart is and always will be. No matter where I will eventually end up it will be home. Even if I am in a corner of a nursing home in some far corner of England I will probably be wearing pyjamas with a Liver Bird logo on them.

It must run in the family – this heritage thing. My dad, John 'Gunner' Grant, came back from his sojourns with the British 8th Army in 1945 to Liverpool and went home only to find that Hitler's bombs had demolished the street. Dad, using that in-built, common sense went to the first place that would hold the answers to the whereabouts of the family. No, not the council offices. He went to the pub, the Liver Hotel in Waterloo.

I didn't want to go to university so, after being taught – and caned regularly – by Christian Brothers, I decided on enjoying Liverpool life and didn't leave home in Liverpool 8 until the age of 26. Then I went off to Ruskin College, Oxford as a mature student. Leaving Lime Street station I realised for the first time looking out of the window of the train, like Pip in *Great Expectations,* that one day I could get back to the place but not the time. I just prayed that the city I was leaving half-built, dirty, broke, a place that had let itself go and was depressed would still be there on return and not be a bombsite – emotional, financial or otherwise – like Dad's war-time home.

Oxford opened my eyes to a world of literature, dreaming spires, Hooray Henrys and Henriettas with more money than sense. But the biggest education was realised at another champagne fuelled party when I was overwhelmed by acute homesickness. I had sat in an arty Oxford cinema watching *Letter to Brezhnev* – a low-budget film made by Liverpool people who wrote, directed and funded it. The opening silent sequence of the Liverpool skyline from a bird's eye view brought me to tears. 'We are just as good as Oxford' I thought as, dream-like, I soared over the Three Graces and saw the two Liver Birds wink at me – which I put down to the pre-screening Guinness. But it was a real longing for that infuriating city. I was missing the people, the buildings, the river and the family.

I moved on again to London and Birmingham, cities that were booming while Liverpool was not.

But in the early to mid 1990s something was happening. A Liver Bird was becoming a Phoenix. I returned home and could see the life support machine had not been switched off. The Mersey monitors were bleeping and there was a growing confidence.

There was colour in the city. When I had left everything was in black and white. It was becoming a renaissance place – the men in suits had vision just like the poets, painters and musicians always had.

Many of those inspirational creative types who made Liverpool famous through their respective talents stayed put.

Willy Russell stayed – his work seen all over the world flying the flag of Liverpool talent. He gave me a homecoming present – a translation of *Blood Brothers* in Japanese. Alan Bleasdale, whose *Boys from the Black Stuff* TV series, is regarded as the mould-breaking dramas series of the 1980s continues to nurture new writers. *The Mersey Sound* – the best-selling poetry anthology from Messrs Adrian Henri, Roger McGough and Brian Patten – was in audiotape form. I once shared a few glasses of Chateau Neuf Du Pape with my then neighbour Adrian Henri. I told him that I never wanted to be a Beatle – I wanted to be a Mersey Poet.

'Go out and do it,' he said. 'Don't go off into the wilderness and never forget you are from Liverpool – you won't go far wrong.'

I lived then in Rodney Street where the author of *The Cruel Sea* Nicholas Monsarrat was born and I daily I marvelled at the architecture. As a journalist celebrating 25 years in the business, I know everything is not rosy but in 21st century Liverpool the positive outshines the negative.

When Colin McKeown, producer of many TV series and films including *Liverpool One* makes a movie he always includes a Liverpool scene. He told me: 'It is my home and I want to show that home in all its glory. It's my lucky charm – that waterfront

Peter Grant was born in Liverpool and educated at Cardinal Godfrey School in Anfield and later at Ruskin College Oxford, where he gained a Diploma in English Literature and Public Speaking. He has worked in all branches of the media – in print for newspapers and magazines, national and provincial: based variously in London, Chester and Birmingham. In radio he has worked as a producer for Radio City in Liverpool and he regularly broadcasts on BBC Radio Merseyside and has appeared on BBC Radio 4's Today programme. He has written extensively on show business, television and the arts for more than 25 years and is now an acknowledged artist in his own right. His first art exhibition *Peter's Lane: The Poartry and Art of Peter Grant* took place in December 2002 at the Mathew Street View gallery. Peter is currently the award-winning TV editor of the *Liverpool Echo*. He lives amidst the leafy glades of St Michaels-in-the-Hamlet in south Liverpool. He is an expert on the life of the Beatles and regularly gives lectures on the Fab Four, plays music, swims and drinks Guinness ... but not at the same time.

scene in a film is like a postcard to the rest of the country – to the universe.' Author Brian Jacques is one of the top children's authors in the world with his Redwall creations. Brian just looks at you painfully when you ask him why he never left Liverpool. 'Are you mad? It's home. Why go anywhere else when we've got it all.'

Singer Gerry Marsden, celebrating 40 years at the top, says that in his song *Ferry 'Cross the Mersey* the words are still so relevant. 'Here is where I always will stay.'

Why does Paul McCartney love home? 'Liverpool put my feet on the ground; it made me what I am. I am from Liverpool and being from Liverpool holds certain responsibilities,' he told me, reflecting on the motto from his old school, now the world-famous Liverpool Institute for Performing Arts' where he gives out the degree badges personally every year.

For me, home has made me what I am today: 'Ah, la, so Liverpool's to blame,' I can hear Gunner Grant say from high up in heaven. He beat the Germans but he couldn't fight Alzheimer's any more. His ashes are in the Mersey.

Now all that literature and arts stuff I grew up with is paying off for me. I had my own art and poetry exhibition at the View 2 gallery in Mathew Street – opened by Willy Russell and with my family, friends and mentors such as Alan Bleasdale and Jimmy McGovern drinking my success along with other actors and musicians. Yeah, yeah, yeah ... I was home that night.

My brother Michael told me a tale soon after he had just returned from a once-in-a-lifetime trip to Kenya. At one beautiful sunset he stood on a veranda and listened to the wildlife; felt the breeze and sipped a cocktail. An African warrior in full native dress with tribal face paint, spear and shield stood next to him.

Michael said he realised then, for a brief magical moment, that there were other places than Liverpool ... than home.

The native tuned to him, smiled and nudged him and said: 'Well, my friend – how is the river Mersey?' Now that's what I call heritage.

The façade of the former (British Rail-owned)
North Western Hotel in Lime Street;
opened in 1871 as Lime Street Chambers it was designed
by Alfred Waterhouse.

'In a harsh environment, where the skills of survival sometimes take precedence over social graces, there ... develops an innate sense of natural justice.'

Phil Redmond

see essay page 94

Informing Visitors About Liverpool's
Part in the Global Tapestry

by Stephen Binns

There are times when I'm conscious that the visitors I am taking around the city are astonished at my unexpected perception; those occasions when I've casually pointed out details that they hadn't noticed, such as the frayed trouser leg on the statue of Prince Albert. In a way it throws them completely because it's fairly obvious I am blind.

But I love doing that kind of thing because it is part of the fun and more surprising aspects of my job as a city tour guide. What they don't know is that I have learned about the city by mood and atmosphere as much as by in-depth research. So, although I might not be able to see, I do know my Liverpool.

And I am a natural entertainer and love 'being in charge' of people in a sense, something that as a disabled person I am aware doesn't tend to happen; it's usually the other way round.

I do believe that I have a better book collection on Liverpool than most of the city's branch libraries, arguably most of the foundation works. And it seems I have the largest Braille library in private hands, according to the people who deal with these matters: close to 3,000 volumes.

Mind you, I couldn't do this without the sterling help from my small team of dedicated researchers who read the books to me, and then put many of them on tape. They are supported by a government grant and, to be honest, I couldn't manage without them.

I'm really proud of my book collection, and certainly my material on William Gladstone – a Liverpool man who was three times prime minister of Britain – is as good as anyone's in the country. I've even been involved in television documentaries about him and have a big bronze bust of him on my office windowsill.

This job came about largely by circumstance and chance because when I started as a guide for the Lord Mayor at the Town Hall – about 14 years ago – no one else really wanted to do it. Indeed, the public didn't use the Town Hall that much at the time and there weren't that many visitors.

After St George's Hall gradually began to reopen after 1992 I took a few groups around it but, by then realising the potential, I wanted to talk to more people about the city. So I toured around schools, day centres and residential care homes. The reception was always enthusiastic.

Soon I was invited on to BBC Radio Merseyside to talk about local people of interest and celebrity; at first with Linda McDermott on her morning show and later with Roger Phillips at lunchtime. I think

I've notched up more than 300 profiles of well known – and not so well known – Scousers of note; and I've got a further 1,000 in my files. I call the project *Raising the Dead* and I believe these people are an essential part of our heritage and deserve a mention; not all have statues or commemorations to them.

It is a wonderful job for me, as I've always loved history. But I was never that interested in local history, thinking it far too parochial. My mind was set on the grander and wider European and world panoramas: the French Revolution and the Spanish Civil War.

But as I dug deeper into Liverpool's past I learned that it is, in fact, a part of that great global tapestry; not the centre of the universe, as so many like to assume, but we have certainly made a remarkable contribution, and an ongoing one. That we have been knocked down repeatedly and yet come bouncing back is fascinating.

I've met people from all over the world and was highly amused – and not a little bemused – when told a few years ago that I'd been voted by a group of Australian tourists as the seventh best attraction in Britain. It seems a bunch of boy scouts from Queensland had been on one of my tours. They appeared on a local radio station in Brisbane and rated me ahead of Windsor Castle and just behind the Houses of Parliament!

Over the years Liverpool has taken the brunt of the critics; sometimes loved, sometimes hated, but never ignored. I was born in the city and attended the oldest blind school in the world in Wavertree. After that I was despatched to Manchester and then, in the late 1960s, to what was oddly termed the Royal Normal College in Shrewsbury.

When I finally left school there were only two kinds of job open to blind people: piano tuning or typing. I didn't fancy the latter and don't have that much of an ear for music so I ended up

Stephen Binns is Liverpool city council's community historian. He was awarded an MBE in the 2004 Queen's Birthday Honours List, for services to heritage. He was born in Liverpool in 1952 and educated variously at schools in the city, Manchester and Shrewsbury. He joined the city council in the then public relations office in 1990. He is now acknowledged as one of the leading experts on Liverpool's history and sites of interest.

making radiator brackets at the old KME factory in Kirkby. Ironically the union convenor there was Jack Spriggs, whom I knew well, neither of us realising that years later I would work for him when he did a stint as Lord Mayor of Liverpool.

Later, when KME closed I went to work for the blind in Cornwallis Street – there simply weren't any other jobs for me – and ended up making doormats. I became an official with the National Union of the Blind and Disabled, one of the then oldest unions in the Trades Union Congress. As a result it was there that I picked up a bit on public speaking and learned about travelling around independently, finding my own way to work and to conferences all over Britain.

When that workshop also closed in 1990 I took up the cudgels on behalf of my colleagues and helped launch a campaign for the local authority to find us jobs; we were all determined to make our own way. I can recall addressing the full council in the Town Hall with the petition, although I didn't have a clue about its history or what an impact the building would have on my life.

Two months later I was working in the council's public relations department and undertook my first tour of the Town Hall in the November of that same year. And I realised that it was going to be a lot of fun. Now I do tours on request, sometimes as many as 20 in a week, and give maybe around 250 talks a year. The variety of the audiences is probably wider than most academic speakers: I've talked about Liverpool's history and heritage in the same day to groups of people aged from five to 85.

What strikes me forcibly about Liverpool is that it always seems to resurrect itself, and this time it feels pretty permanent. As the city council's community historian I find it truly exciting that we can appear now in the same list of astonishing structures such as the Pyramids at Giza or the great Inca cities of old. It doesn't mean we are any better, or any worse, but the very idea that we are on equal footing with these remarkable places across the world is breathtaking.

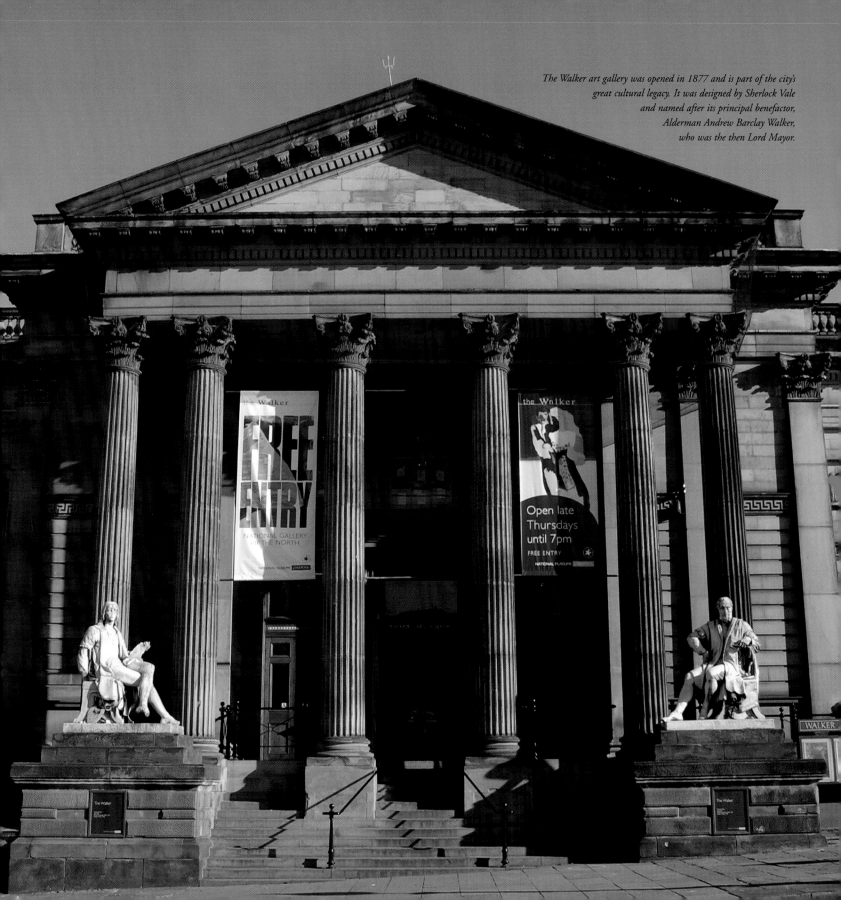

The Walker art gallery was opened in 1877 and is part of the city's
great cultural legacy. It was designed by Sherlock Vale
and named after its principal benefactor,
Alderman Andrew Barclay Walker,
who was the then Lord Mayor.

'A place which
once again believed
that the mantle of
the merchant princes
of Florence had fallen
upon its shoulders'

Joe Riley

see essay page 144

Left: A young Queen Victoria on horseback located on St George's Hall plateau. A bronze by Thomas Thornycroft, it was erected in 1870.

Examples of Liverpool's architectural gems

Lime Street Station, 1867–79, *Grade II*

St George's Hall, 1840–55, *Grade I*

William Brown Museum and Library, 1857–60, *Grade II**

Lime Street Chambers (former North Western Hotel), opened 1871, *Grade II*

Walker Art Gallery, opened 1877, *Grade II**

Picton Reading Room and Hornby Library, 1875–9 and 1906, *Grade II**

County Sessions House, 1882–4, *Grade II**

College of Technology and Museum Extension, 1896–1901, *Grade II**

The Wellington Memorial (1861–3) and the Steble Fountain (1877–9), *Grade II**

Monuments on St George's Plateau

St John's Gardens and its Monuments

Empire Theatre, 1925, *Grade II*

Entrance to the Mersey Tunnel, 1925–34, *Grade II*

The Cultural
Living Zone

zone 6

'the city's
waterfront renaissance
sets a benchmark
for design excellence;
it sets a
world-class standard
for the future.'

Jim Gill

see essay page 212

The Cultural Shock that
Turned into a Cultural Joy

by Phil Key

It was a grey, chilly morning when I stepped off the London train at Lime Street station in late November 1968. I had arrived to work as a night reporter on the *Liverpool Daily Post* and, apart from the one visit for the job interview, this was to be my introduction to Liverpool.

The station was looking decidedly down-at-heel, as was the nearby public house to which I retired to meet the locals. 'What are you doing here?' demanded one man at the bar on hearing my London accent. 'You don't fit in with that voice.' I wandered the city with my suitcase as I had a few hours to spare before meeting the friends who had promised to put me up at their Sefton Park flat. It was a discouraging sight, with many of the buildings grime-encrusted and the shoppers glum-faced.

At least there was a cheery reception from my friends, although it was clear they had very little space and I would have to rent a place of my own. The next day I went flat hunting, after explaining my needs to an agency. The first place they sent me to had a missing window pane with a piece of dirty matting nailed in place to cover the gap. If that appalled me, I was even more surprised when I visited a south Liverpool butcher's shop to buy some provisions. It featured a prominent sign announcing 'No Spitting in this Establishment'. What sort of people would need such a warning, I wondered?

The weather remained bleak, as did my prospects of staying in Liverpool for more than a few months. The job was fine but I thought I would be back in London within a year. Well, I never did go back.

Looking back now, I realise what a conceited little twerp I must have been back then. I had arrived in Liverpool with all the arrogance of a southerner who thought it must be grim 'Up North'. After all, in London where I had worked on local newspapers for some years I had access to all the best theatres and art galleries. I was a regular at the Royal Court theatre in Chelsea, had seen Noel Coward on stage and even enjoyed a camp evening watching John Hanson in *The Desert Song*. The National Gallery was like a second home and I could buy all the jazz records and books I wanted in Charing Cross Road.

Later I had gone to work in Tripoli, Libya, editing the *Daily News of Tripoli,* a role that now sounds better than it was. I had to write the whole newspaper, edit it and see it to 'bed', the newspaper production term for getting the paper onto the press – all in a building that had no air conditioning and in temperatures that were regularly over 100F. At this stage King Idris was still on the throne and there was a relaxed

atmosphere about the country so while I worked hard, I also played hard in the night clubs. Excess finally took its toll and I returned home to south London to look for a job. Unexpectedly, Liverpool beckoned.

It was a cultural shock I must admit and there were some things I never did get used to, like the way people then would regularly spit in the street.

But what I did soon discover was that Liverpool had a cultural life all its own. Very soon I had forgotten the theatres and galleries of London while I discovered those in Liverpool. The Everyman was going through a golden age; the Liverpool Playhouse was doing great business, as were the Royal Court and the Empire theatres. The Walker art gallery was a real eye-opener and there was a busy arts community. I was soon on the reviewing list of the *Liverpool Daily Post* as an extra to my normal reporting duties. For a while I worked as industrial correspondent, a period when I was able to observe first hand a sad decline in a great city, as factories closed and jobs were lost.

A move to writing a daily light-hearted diary column lifted my spirits as I realised that the people of Liverpool were never going to get down-hearted. There were always stories of people coming up with new employment ideas, writing plays, playing in bands, opening shops, taking to the stage, painting, creating festivals or making furniture ... the list was endless.

My appointment as arts correspondent, later arts editor, was to reinforce this message. Whatever the news headlines might say, the cultural heritage of Liverpool was there for all to see. When I first arrived not everyone was willing to see it. This was the era after they had just knocked down the Cavern club and a Liverpool councillor had famously declared that the Beatles 'could not sing for toffee'. Historic buildings were being torn down with gay abandon. Even the region's major arts organisation, the

Philip Key was born in Penge, south London close on 60 years ago and began his career on the *Kentish Times*. He then headed off to Libya to edit an English language paper in Tripoli. He returned to the UK a year later to the maelstrom of news gathering and reporting. He came to Liverpool some 37 years ago to take up a position as night reporter on the *Daily Post* but his abilities at 'digging out' the gossip gave him the chance to write a distinctive daily diary column, a job that lasted five years. After a spell as features editor he found his true niche on the arts desk. Phil is considered one of the last proper 'characters' in a newspaper industry that now demands certain conformity. After more than a quarter of a century as arts editor covering the *Daily Post's* wide circulation around Merseyside and North Wales he is rated by many as the doyen of drama and culture; his particular favourite muses include dance and opera. He is also an avid reader and boasts a collection of more than 2,000 books, mostly on murder because Phil cherishes a passion for crime thrillers and whodunits.

Merseyside Arts Association, was often torn apart by internal strife. There came a gradual realisation that Liverpool had a heritage of which it could be proud – including the Beatles. Perhaps it was the writers who established it best. Television dramas like *Z Cars* and comedies such as *The Liver Birds* brought the city's particular style into living rooms across the country. In the theatres, Willy Russell and Alan Bleasdale were making a terrific impact. Even in clubland, a club like Eric's, which fostered the early punk bands, was making its own contribution not only to Liverpool's culture but that of the country. I was a regular and, even though rather too old and more conservatively dressed than most customers, I was accepted and joined in that exciting musical movement.

Young artists who had been leaving the city had now decided to stay as a series of artists' studios opened across the city and there was for a while a revival of the Liverpool Academy of Arts. Tate Liverpool was a watershed, making Liverpool one of the most vibrant centres for visual art.

One event seemed to sum up the new mood, the first night of Willy Russell's *Blood Brothers* at the Liverpool Playhouse in 1983. I had originally watched *Blood Brothers* as a one-hour play performed in a school hall by the Merseyside Young People's Theatre Company. Even at that stage I realised that Russell had written a classic. Extended with Russell's music and a wonderful cast led by Barbara Dickson, it was a revelation. On that opening night, the audience rose as one to cheer the show to the rafters. I was later to see it premiered in the West End and on Broadway, where the reaction was exactly the same.

Along with its new sense of cultural identity, Liverpool began looking at the city itself. The International Garden Festival brought a new sense of purpose, buildings were improved rather than knocked down and most of the grime was finally scraped away. Today, visitors arriving at Lime Street station will find a cleaner, more dynamic place than I did in 1968, the city itself rather jaunty. The history remains, the never-say-die spirit remains, the cultural heritage remains.

And, of course, I have remained.

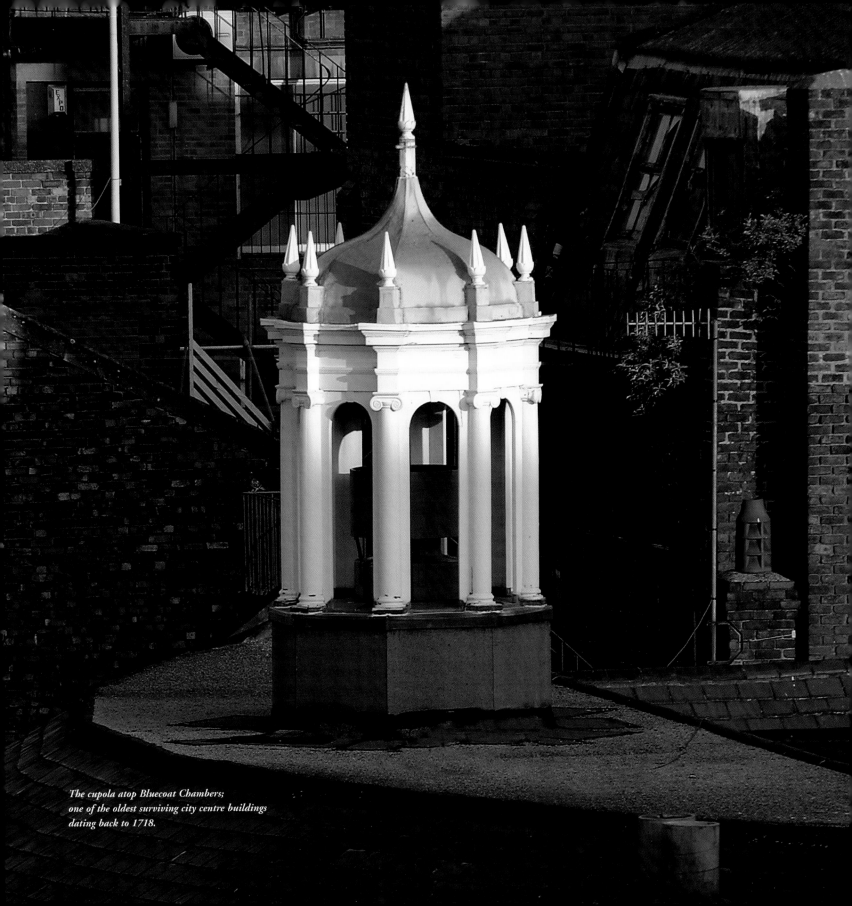

The cupola atop Bluecoat Chambers;
one of the oldest surviving city centre buildings
dating back to 1718.

'Even if I am in
a nursing home ... in
some far corner of
England I will probably
be wearing pyjamas
with a Liver Bird logo ...'

Peter Grant

see essay page 158

China Connections Add Spice
to Liverpool's International Flavour

by Lew Baxter

There is a piquant hint of intriguing chance, maybe even destiny, that the decision about Liverpool's World Heritage status should have been announced in Suzhou. This ancient and lovely Chinese canal city – nestling near the banks of the glorious Lake Taihu – is a neighbour of Shanghai which became a sister city to Liverpool in October 1999, only a week after the 50th anniversary of the establishment of the People's Republic of China.

That twinning agreement is hugely symbolic of the close and historical ties not only with China's largest city – conservative estimates put the number of people working and living in this throbbing, stimulating metropolis at 15 million, and growing exponentially – but also of the two nations, probably more so as a significant number of Liverpool's Chinese citizens can trace their origins back to Shanghai.

Today an awe-inspiring Ceremonial Arch is located in Liverpool's Chinatown to underpin that special relationship. Although located just outwith of the World Heritage parameters, this striking and colourful structure is both an architectural and tourism icon in Liverpool, heralding a new era of friendship and cooperation between the city and Shanghai, now acknowledged as one of Asia's most dynamic 21st century cities.

It is argued with a degree of reality that Liverpool's Chinese community is the oldest in Europe; traced back to wandering seafarers making the bustling seaport their home in the 1880s, although the exact date of the earliest settlement is shaded to inscrutability by the spectres of age and misty memories.

According to Maria Lin Wong, author of the definitive history *Chinese Liverpudlians,* it is believed that the Chinese community in Liverpool actually came about partly after the founding of the Ocean Steam Ship Company in 1865, or more specifically the Blue Funnel Line, the company behind the first direct steamship link between Britain and China.

In this new century the city of Liverpool proper is home to little more than 3,000 people who came directly themselves – or have close family relatives – from a China that is determinedly proud of a cultural history stretching back 5,000 years, and a contemporary population verging on 1.3 billion. But the proportionately tiny Liverpool Chinese clan – although demographically larger across the region *per se,* possibly as many as 10,000 people – displays a unique and bonding pride in their joint 'homelands'. And, of course, China boasts numerous and grandiose World Heritage sites; some perhaps conceived when Liverpool was in the midst of metamorphosing from a fledgling hamlet on the river Mersey into a maritime city of worldwide prominence.

It is recorded that around 1918 there were about 3,200 Chinese men living on shore in Liverpool, the majority associated in some way with seafaring. Yet by the 1930s the community unfathomably dwindled – like all other Chinese communities in Britain – and the Census Report showed there were only 529 Chinese nationals living in the area at one point, and this figure included any British born wives.

What isn't in any dispute is that the Chinese community in Liverpool expanded dramatically in the 1940s, as a result of both World War II and to an extent the turmoil of the infamous Japanese invasion of China in the mid 1930s.

Many people, mostly men, escaped the disruption or couldn't return to China once the Japanese had occupied all the treaty ports in the early 1940s, while others later also fled from the political and social upheaval as Mao Tse-Tung led the Communists in a desperate civil war against the Kuomintang, now referred to as Guomindang in the modern Putonghua parlance.

As World War II continued furiously through the early 1940s Liverpool was the headquarters of the Western Approaches that monitored and defended the Atlantic, guarding the vital supply sea-lanes. After years of arduous warfare and lost ships and crews, the Merchant Navy was desperate for seamen and embarked on a worldwide recruiting drive among Britain's allies. Thus the city also became home to the Chinese Merchant Seamen's Pool, which resulted in thousands of Chinese sailors landing in the port. At one stage it is estimated there were around 20,000 registered Chinese sailors, a considerable number hailing from Shanghai, with others from various parts of mainland China.

A Personal View: That Feeling Called Home

Tseng Chihkao reflects fondly on Liverpool

Early in 1945, a young Chinese man barely 20 years of age found himself in a war-battered Liverpool, a strangely exotic and wildly foreign city to his Oriental eyes. He spoke hardly any English apart from a few random words he had picked up in Calcutta, and had been transported in a troop ship – the *Empress of Canada* – from India to join the vitally needed pool of Chinese seamen who were to help revive Britain's bruised merchant fleet.

Despite the nature of the circumstances he was nervously excited to be in the country that he heard so much about as a boy in his rural home close to the Yangtze River, deep in the province of Sichuan. Now 79 years of age Tseng Chihkao has spent all of his adult life in Liverpool; it is approaching six decades but it might be a year or two more as he admits official records are vague. He chuckles good-humouredly that even after all that time many of his British friends can't pronounce his name; they know him familiarly yet with great affection simply as San.

Young Tseng was forced to leave China when he was merely 16 or 17; his family scattered far and wide because of the Japanese War that had ravaged both the cities and the vast countryside, the cruelties now embalmed in the darkest of folklore. After Pearl Harbour and the American intervention in World War II, Tseng Chihkao was drafted into the Chinese army – it was then under the control of Chiang Kai-shek – that was joining forces with the British and American armies in the struggle against Japan in Burma. 'I was flown to Nepal for six months' training, although I must admit a little reluctantly. Then along with thousands of other Chinese soldiers I was assigned to the Burmese front line in late 1941,' recalled Tseng who spent 18 months in the heat of battle. He was wounded twice and on the second occasion, after being discharged from a field hospital, he discovered his regiment had moved on, constantly seeking out the enemy in the jungles.

'I was quite weak and couldn't catch them up and I was invalided out of the army because of my wounds. Returning to China was still out of the question and I was flown to Calcutta, where I got a job as a waiter in a Chinese restaurant. There I spotted an advertisement for the British Merchant Navy, which was looking for seamen. I applied, although I didn't hold out much hope as I was quite small. But to my utter surprise I was accepted by the Blue Funnel Line and shipped back to England,' commented Tseng, who reveals that although he had no English, he spoke fluent Hindustani, Mandarin and several Chinese dialects; linguistic skills that have proved their worth in latter years.

'I was so grateful to arrive in Liverpool; in England. Back in my hometown we had often talked of this mysterious, faraway land but I never imagined I would end up here. 'Where I was actually born doesn't mean that much to me now, although I am of course very proud to be Chinese; it's just that my family had long since dispersed. I regard Liverpool as my home, even if my heart is still in China.'

WELCOME TO SAN'S

HOME COOKED

QUALITY CAFE FOOD

CAF

For 20 years Tseng worked for the Blue Funnel Line, traversing the globe as a seaman, visiting most countries but always returning to his British wife Joan and growing family in Liverpool; he now has six children, the oldest is 39 and the youngest 33. 'Joan is from Yorkshire and was working in a factory in Liverpool during the war, that's how I met her. My family are fascinated by my story and I do feel lucky that out of the millions of Chinese people who suffered from the wars and unrest of that period, I survived and thrived.'

After being made redundant by Blue Funnel Line in 1965, Tseng turned his hand to working part-time in a Chinese restaurant in Manchester and as a casual docker on the Liverpool and Birkenhead docks, part of a shore gang as he recalls; a system of shameful arbitrary employment that has thankfully long since been abandoned.

At that time, in order to look after his family, Tseng opened a small café on the docksides rustling up the fiery yet tasty food of his native Sichuan and other more homely – some might suggest bland – British fayre. Today San's Café is a popular and regular haunt of an eclectic mix of customers: seafarers, lorry drivers, dockworkers and the local business community, all keen to sample his blend of Chinese and British food; he even provides a sandwich delivery service. His work ethic demands that he continues to put in a seven-day week, helped by his wife and three of the children.

'Of course, I have noticed many changes in Liverpool since I came here, essentially as a boy. And I am really proud that the city has taken off and that it has World Heritage status, especially as it was announced in China, and not that far from where I was born. I suppose now I am half Sichuanese and half Scouser,' added Tseng, whose English is delightfully infused with the guttural, nasal twang of the true Liverpudlian.

Tseng first went back to China to trace his relatives in 1958, before the now accepted insanity of the Cultural Revolution closed the country down again, and did find most of his sisters and brothers. He didn't get to return to the Middle Kingdom again until 1982 when the political situation had calmed; although he regrets that neither his wife nor children have ever visited China. One day they will, he hopes.

These days he tries to make a visit every couple of years and now also works as an advisor to several British companies doing business in China, notably the Liverpool Water Witch Company that makes marine pollution control vessels. He often assists the Liverpool Chamber of Commerce's China Link organisation, headed up by his friend Wu Kegang, an economist and a driving force in Liverpool's links with China. And after 55 years as a member, Tseng is now very proud of being deputy chairman of the UK Chinese Freemasons, an important and influential networking group.

'I am delighted that Liverpool is twinned with Shanghai and now that China has really opened up I am able to go back freely and have made many new friends there. I am treated like a VIP. But I am always glad to be back in Liverpool where I have been consistently shown warmth and respect by everybody from the Lord Mayor down.'

Liverpool's spectacular Chinese Arch representing the friendship and close links with its twin city of Shanghai: it was completed and erected in September 2000.

Champagne and Cheers Greeted Liverpool Winning European Capital of Culture

by Laura Davis

The news that Liverpool had won European Capital of Culture rippled across the city like a fast flowing current in the river Mersey.

There were those who had heard the original announcement while walking to work, listening to arts minister Tessa Jowell's words on portable radios they did not usually carry. Others received the happy tidings by email, sent to the entire staff of some of the city's major companies by their normally faceless management.

Commuters, many of whom had already heard it whispered from carriage to carriage, were greeted on their arrival at Liverpool's city centre railway stations by hand-made signs waved by ordinarily surly guards. By 8.30am – the announcement had been made at 8.10am – shopkeepers across the city had placed word-processed *'Congratulations Liverpool!'* posters in their windows. An hour later, when the reluctant disbelief had passed, there was a sense of excitement and community reminiscent of a Silver Jubilee street party.

But the reason for the celebration – the reason a double decker bus driver would later stop his vehicle in the middle of a busy road and get out to shake bid leader Sir Bob Scott's hand – was not that Liverpool was a capital of culture. It was that people across the country, normally so quick to criticise, would finally have to acknowledge it. At the same moment members of the winning bid team were popping open their first bottle of champagne, editors of every national newspaper in the country were wishing they had a reporter in Liverpool. As the city rushed to make arrangements for Jowell's arrival at Lime Street station later that morning, Merseyside property agents found themselves bombarded by telephone calls from southern investors looking to buy up whole streets of houses in the region. Within the past 12 months, it has suddenly become the norm to see Liverpool alongside Knightsbridge and Edinburgh in national magazine articles about fashionable shopping, wining and dining destinations. Before last June, Manchester was consistently chosen as the token North West city to be featured by the glossies. National and international organisations are now realising Liverpool's potential, noting that the European title and this World Heritage nomination have turned it into a no-risk option for investment.

Channel Five has chosen the city as the first to be featured in its Five Arts Cities project that will see Merseyside galleries and creative people profiled in a series of television programmes.

190

Organisers of the Tall Ships race, equally impressed by the grand welcome Liverpool people gave to last year's Clipper Round the World Yacht Race, the city's Capital of Culture win and its nomination as World Heritage site, have elected to hold the high profile event along its waterfront in July 2008. And, perhaps most delightful of all, author Jonathan Margolis, who branded Liverpool *'Self-Pity City'* following the murder of James Bulger, finally admitted he was wrong.

Capital of Culture has given a sense of pride back to the people of this city. A pride in an identity that has nothing to do with comedians' curly, black wigs, unflattering leisurewear or police wearing riot gear. But what is Capital of Culture really? Simply a few words attached to a city for 12 months. It brings little monetary benefit by itself – just a small pot of Euros from the European Commission.

Yet the excitement surrounding 2008 is unique. No other country has experienced such a fiercely fought competition for the title and, consequently, it appears that Liverpool's year of celebrations will stand out. The enthusiasm for the title, and for its holder, has been generated from within, and the city is about to reap the benefits.

One of the questions the judging panel asked all six short-listed cities was how they would promote themselves to foreign journalists. Liverpool's bid team replied that they would say they were offering the chance of a lifetime, to witness one of the world's most spectacular cities turning its luck around. To be able to say they had been among the few to see Liverpool's potential and tip it as one of the major tourist destinations of the future when others were still making jibes about stealing car wheels.

Well, Liverpool people have all been in that privileged position for years now. It's finally time to say: 'I told you so.' And this World Heritage title is the icing on the cake.

A graduate of Leeds University, where she cut her teeth on the student newspaper, Laura Davis returned to the city of her birth in September 2000, as a business reporter for the *Liverpool Daily Post*. Offered a position in the newsroom around a year later, she took over the newspaper's coverage of the city's bid for European Capital of Culture. She reported on plans for 2008, trailing after the judging panel as they made their inspections of Liverpool's arts and community attractions. Laura now writes a weekly page on the lead up to 2008 and is a major contributor to the *Daily Post's Cultural Quarterly* magazine.

'... I thought ... I should ... sit and drink in sad old pubs and dirty places.'

'[Now] there is a remarkable buzz that was lacking before ...'

Lisa McMullan & Maggie O'Carroll

see essay page 128

Why the World Must Learn to Live in Peace and Become Truly One World in All Cities

by Saranda Hajdari

Even though I was born and grew up in what we thought of as an occupied country our family had been really happy. My dad is an ethnic Albanian and my mum a Kosovan Albanian. She likes to call me by the pet name of Landa.

My three sisters, Shqipdona, Almedina and Irsa and my brother Endrit were all born in the village, and now we have a new sister – Lanika – who was born in Liverpool in Britain.

Our troubles really began in the summer of 1999. The fighting started because some people wanted only pure Serbians living in certain regions. Serbia wanted to take over Kosovo but the Kosovans wouldn't let that happen; and the war started.

My dad was a highly respected primary school teacher and my mum a brilliant fashion designer with her own shop, and we were an ordinary middle-class family. I can still remember how my dad would sit and help me with my homework every night, and how during the day we played happily with our cousins.

Then it all changed. In the middle of the night, mum woke us up and I heard loud noises. At first I thought it was something exciting, but it wasn't. The police were shooting at the houses. Mum, dad and us five children had to creep out and run for safety to our uncle's house further down the street.

Every night for the next few days we stayed in our uncle's cellar, covered by quilts and pillows. The women and children remained hidden, whilst the men stood on guard. The whole street was in that room! It was full of women and children. I was always glad to get out because it was so stuffy. The bombings were so bad that I didn't know if I was going to make it through till morning.

We wore all our clothes in case we had to leave and could travel faster. Everyone did the same. We were ordered to black out the windows and tape them up to prevent flying glass during a bomb explosion. That became part of the pattern of daily life, under constant threat of attack. Exhaustion, lack of sleep, fear of dying; these were just everyone's feelings, every day. The bombings were really bad and if the city being destroyed wasn't bad enough, I often thought I had gone through an earthquake as my whole body and mind would shake.

Even if you weren't in danger of being killed by a bomb, then you were in danger of a threat of attack. Serbian soldiers used to go into houses by force and shout to the people: 'If you don't evacuate the city within the hour, you will all be dead meat.' We were all scared to death. Then one day the thing we feared most happened to us. Confronted by a group of soldiers, we froze. It seemed unreal, almost like a dream. We didn't want to believe it but unfortunately it was reality, and we all had to face it.

After issuing their threats, my dad quickly decided that we should leave immediately ... so we did. When we left our home, we were on the move a lot, staying in different houses. One day, when we were playing outside our latest temporary home, Serbian soldiers approached. I ran to the house to warn the grown-up but it was too late. The soldiers marched in, thinking they were gods. In their camouflage uniforms they entered like giants covered in paint. Once again we froze.

A soldier shouted: 'Don't move!' I thought that he was going to kill us all. Our parents were coming out of the house; I remember that my dad had my little brother in his arms. A soldier snatched my brother out of my dad's arms and another soldier grabbed my dad and dragged him out of the gates. My brother started crying. My dad looked at me and said: 'Don't worry.' And he promised he would come back shortly. I couldn't even cry because the soldiers wouldn't let us. If I did, it would have made things worse for father. They arrested him and took him away to prison. The rest of the soldiers then ransacked our house. They took all the precious things from my mother's handbag, our birth certificates, passports, money and jewellery. They took my dad, and the rest of the survivors were just waiting to be shot. Even though I didn't get killed, since that day, to me, my soul was killed. My life ended there.

But dad escaped from prison after three days, three nights, six hours and 15 minutes. My daddy returned to me but was unrecognisable. He said to me: 'I told you, I will always keep my promise.'

Saranda Hajdari is a youth advisor for UNICEF in Britain. She is an apparently well-balanced 15-year-old and a pupil at St Hilda's school in Liverpool's Sefton Park, close to where she now lives. Yet she was born in the small village of Gjilan, in the province of Presheva in southern Serbia, close to the border with Kosovo. Her family was forced to flee their war-ravaged homeland in 1999, to find sanctuary in Britain: albeit that the family's permanent residency is subject to Home Office approval. When they landed in Liverpool none spoke any English but Saranda rapidly picked up on the 'Scouse' *lingua franca* and has been the family's real lifeline to starting a new life, as they struggled to put the horrific past behind them. Despite her tender years she has become something of a celebrity in Liverpool, has featured in the city council's publications and joined the UK focused Youth Voice. She lives with her mother Nazlije and father Ekrem, along with five younger brothers and sisters – Shqipdona, Almedina, Endrit, Irsa and one-month-old Lanika. This is her story, in her own words.

When he came back, we packed up what we could and set off for a safer area of Presheva. But as soon as we got to one safe place, the soldiers would arrive and drive us all out again.

Eventually mum and dad decided that even though the stories of what the camps were like in Macedonia were horrifying, we would have to walk many, many miles to get there simply because it was the only safe place. By this time mum, dad and us five children – aged between six months and eight years old – only had what we stood up in and a massive bag of other precious clothes and blankets. Mum carried my baby sister and dad, even though he had this huge bag, half carried an old woman who could barely walk.

As we fled from the soldiers, some of the women found that they couldn't carry their babies anymore. So they hid them in rocks and left them behind. I was terrified that mum would do the same with my baby sister, but fortunately she had the strength to keep on going. During my journey, I experienced seeing people already killed, people being killed, people being burnt and people being cut into pieces. Sometimes I wonder how I survived all of this, not just physically but mentally.

Eventually, after endless days of walking, we arrived at the refugee camp in Macedonia but pretty soon we realised how bad things were. Although we had food, it was very basic and I know this sounds bad, but our family had been quite wealthy, and we were not used to eating just bread and milk. We felt like prisoners but at least we were safe. After six weeks we were shown a list of countries that had agreed to accept Kosovans like us.

One of them was England. All I knew about England was that it is in the middle of the sea and the people were crazy about football. But at least we would be welcomed rather than shot at.

After first flying to Leeds Airport we arrived by bus in Liverpool, and it was the first time in my whole life that my family and I felt free. It was the first time that we took a deep breath and smelt the freedom of life.

Coming to England was the best day of my life. You see, I didn't read about a war, watch a documentary on the war or even hear about it ... I experienced it! I was part of the war; I was a victim in some ways. War does terrible things. Kosovo had a beautiful culture and way of life but, like a flower whose roots have been damaged, it will never be the same again. I remember seeing a photograph of mum and dad before all the troubles. They looked so happy, but I don't think they'll ever look like that again. How can they?

My message to everyone is this: if you are given just enough time and just enough money to live in peace, then be thankful and live that time to the full. I also hope that you are always safe and that you always have friends. I hope that nobody looks at you and calls you bad names for no other reason than that you are different.

I think we children have adjusted well and have learned English. We made friends quite easily and I think that our terrible experiences meant we could stand on our own two feet. Now I am in secondary school and I have a pretty good Liverpool accent. I am ambitious to become an international businesswoman.

I arrived here not knowing who I was or who I was going to be. But five years later I am a different person. Liverpool was, is and will be a paradise for me because in this city I have found friends, a school and, more importantly, myself. I hope to stay here and go to university. Even if the Home Office eventually insists that our family returns to Kosovo, it will never be able to take Liverpool out of me!

'... after a while,
it felt like it was time
to come home.
Liverpool is my home;
... it is part of
my culture.'

Barbara Smith

see essay page 104

Examples of Liverpool's architectural gems

Bluecoat Chambers, School Lane, opened 1718, *Grade I*

Thomas Parr's House and Warehouse, Colquitt Street, 1799, *Grade II*

Warehouse at 33 Argyle Street/14–18 Henry Street, late 19th century, *Grade II*

105 Duke Street, c.1800, *Grade II*

The Bridewell (Argyle/Campbell Street), 1861, *Grade II*

Warehouse and Offices at 12 Hanover Street, 1863 and 1889, *Grade II*

The Future

'... it is, in the end, extraordinary people willing to go beyond popular and deep-rooted conventions who break die-hard prejudices.'

Gerald John Pillay

see essay page 124

A Tale of Two Cities – Liverpool & Shanghai

by Will Alsop

On my most recent trip to Shanghai I was struck by the parallels between these sister cities, both made great by international trade and each possessing a strong and enduring character. Standing on Liverpool's Pier Head I am reminded of the Old Bund in Shanghai; each is exciting, and displays an outward looking sensibility appropriate to citizens who are used to enjoying worldwide influence and renown.

Of course, there was always a corresponding influx of new ideas and invention to both cities from overseas, and these bold river frontages are evidence of the healthy cultural exchange that has given these places their truly international character and diversity.

Sixteen million people all intent on change – without destruction of their culture – live in Shanghai. It is not a city that immediately appeals although views across the river from the Bund at night transport one to an image of a future city that has more to do with the *Eagle* comic than China; or is it all the more relevant because China ranks as one of the earliest civilisations whose influence on later cultures as they spread to the West was enormous. Does this recent flow of forms, invention and power from the West merely complete a circle of influence back to the very beginnings of the country?

Things undoubtedly happen fast in the city. Pu Dong, on the former 'wrong' side of the river in Shanghai did not exist five years ago and yet recently I ate an Italian lunch on the 56th floor of a tower that boasts 88 and that owes one or two things to Gotham City. As I looked out over the city from my midday sustenance I saw some 2,700 new towers over 25 storeys. I am told that there are another 2,000 with planning permission in the pipeline.

Architecturally, Liverpool is amongst the richest cities in England, and it is a source of great pride for me to add to the continuing heritage. In designing the Fourth Grace for one of the city's most prominent sites, I am aware that a structure which will carry such cultural import should be not only pleasurable but also something of a challenge, both to build and to be part of. This is the spirit of the Fourth Grace, but its manifestation will be a source of renewed distinction and pride for the people in their city and a tangible message to the world of this historic port's endurance in the future. Liverpool is a city I find easy to love.

My acquaintance with Shanghai is growing stronger with each successive visit, and consequently I am in a position to identify in both cities a frankness, an openness to innovation, rooted in a justified self-assurance. China's boom areas are building much faster than those in the West, aided by a lack of

restrictions; from the outside it would appear that only the simplest of strategies for planning could be adopted. If this were not the case, the local authority would not be able to cope. It could be argued, of course, that if they were not able to keep pace with change and simply gave up the result would be better.

Maybe this rush of adrenalin which characterises China at present is its true nature; the massive cultural change is contiguous with the many different influences on this place throughout its history. There are still some half-timbered British suburban houses which now find themselves in a central location thanks to the rapid and haphazard growth of the place. The removal of past historical layering is Shanghai's quality, although the rate of change continues to increase with each passing year. Embracing this, I find myself loving Shanghai and wishing it well; it is the same fondness I have for Liverpool.

Will Alsop was born in Northampton, England in 1947 and studied at the Architectural Association School in London from 1968 to 1973. After graduating he worked at Cedric Price until 1977 and then with Roderick Hamm for a year. With fellow former student John Lyall, he established Alsop & Lyall in 1981, joined later by Jan Stormer. After Lyall left in 1991 the practice was renamed Alsop & Stormer. The firm has offices in London, Rotterdam, Hamburg, Moscow and Shanghai. He is currently a visiting professor at Vienna Technical University. He recently presented the UK Channel 4 television series *Supercities*. His works include Peckham Library and Media Centre, which won the Stirling Prize in 2000; North Greenwich Station in London; Cardiff Bay Visitors' Centre; Hotel du Département des Bouches-du-Rhone; Marseilles local government offices; the Hamburg ferry terminal; and he is currently working on a project in Shanghai. He has also designed the controversial plans for The Cloud at Liverpool's Pier Head, which has been dubbed the Fourth Grace.

Will Alsop views a model of his proposed 'Cloud' at Liverpool's Pier Head.

The Waterfront – Once More a Pool of Life

by Jim Gill

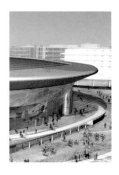

All truly great cities are built on great rivers. They are its lifeblood, a powerful symbol of continuity and often an important source of economic vitality. Inevitably rivers and waterfronts also become the visual frame and definition for a city's sense of identity.

In 1862 the influential Liverpool periodical *The Porcupine* declared: 'Our river is our current of life. Without it, or excluded from it we are simply nothing. But,' the author regaled, 'we treat it as a Sultan treats his wife. We bar it round with walls and gates and obstructions of every kind, and do our utmost possible to prevent the public from ever getting a glimpse of it.'

The campaigning zeal of Victorian opinion formers and their determination 'to open the eyes of our local authorities to the unspeakable importance of improving the approaches to the river' no doubt helped to provide the impetus for the subsequent development of the Three Graces and the creation of the Pier Head as Liverpool's civic hub. As the direct economic significance of the Mersey has declined in recent decades, Liverpool has retreated both physically and psychologically from the water's edge.

In 2000, Liverpool Vision brought in a team of international urban design experts to assist in the preparation of its 'strategic regeneration framework'. The team concluded that the waterfront – and in particular its emotional epicentre, the Pier Head – had become isolated and disconnected from the wider city centre. Access to the river has been inhibited by both physical and cognitive barriers as well as the absence of any compelling public functions or attractions.

For Liverpool Vision the key aim is to reclaim and re-animate the waterfront, making it once again a pool of life, integral to the identity and experience of the new Liverpool.

The designation of the waterfront core as a World Heritage site, is therefore an event of immense significance – an historic opportunity for a city that has for too long 'turned its back' on its most important physical attribute. Water exercises an extraordinary regenerative power. Across the UK and the world, waterfronts have provided the focus and impetus for regeneration. They are immediately attractive and invigorating places to live, work and visit. The World Heritage site designation in no way inhibits or constrains the city's waterfront renaissance. It reinforces our determination to conserve our rich and diverse architectural heritage, but also sets a benchmark and aspiration for quality and design excellence. It quite literally sets a world-class standard for future development.

Liverpool's waterfront must be more than a testimony to the glory and grandeur of a former age; it must also be an equally eloquent statement of future ambition. The *Observer* journalist, Faisal Islam, was amongst many who perceived the importance of Liverpool's extraordinary architectural wealth in securing the European Capital of Culture title. 'Once these ghosts of imperial splendour are integrated into a modern cityscape,' he declared, 'the city will once again shine.' Driving our vision are a series of exciting and ambitious landmark projects that will establish the waterfront as both an international visitor destination and a place that can once again be experienced and enjoyed by the people of Liverpool.

Jim Gill,
chief executive, Liverpool Vision.

Will Alsop's iconic Fourth Grace is a vibrant audacious development housing National Museums Liverpool's definitive 'Museum of Liverpool Life', a powerful and dramatic symbol of Liverpool's re-emergence as a pioneering world city.

Wilkinson Eyre's stunning Arena and Conference Centre will not only provide the city with much needed civic facilities, but will also be the architectural centrepiece of an exciting new urban quarter at King's Waterfront.

However, Vision is looking beyond the obvious 'pull' of these large-scale attractions. Plans for the Pier Head will deliver a new people-friendly environment with dramatically improved pedestrian and public transport links to the wider city centre.

The Pier Head will be an important hub for the Merseytram network as well as the backdrop for British Waterways' hugely imaginative Liverpool Canal Link, a key device that will give unity and animation to the waterfront. Not one of the most architecturally prepossessing developments, but one of the most symbolically potent is the proposed new cruise liner facility earmarked for completion in 2007. The return of the world's greatest cruise ships to one of the world's greatest waterfronts underlines the abiding importance of the river as a recurrent motif in the Liverpool story – a source of our former wealth and prestige, a wellspring for regeneration and future prosperity.

When the first cruise visitors step ashore in 2007 they will be setting foot in a World Heritage site, in a prospective European Capital of Culture celebrating its 700th anniversary. They will also be disembarking in a city that has undergone its own remarkable voyage of transformation – a city that has arrived.

'In almost every sense
Liverpool is
a European city ...
which for good or bad
has helped to shape
world and
European culture.'

Ian Wray

see essay page 134

Part of Liverpool John Moores University's 'Re-animating the Waterfront' project.

Award-winning pedestrian bridge at Princes Dock, designed by Liverpool John Moores University architecture student Ed Ross.

How the Young Architects of the Future
Envisage Liverpool's Waterfront

In many ways the 'untamed' Scouser spirit is emerging triumphant again, so writes Dr Athanassios Migos, senior lecturer in architecture at Liverpool John Moores University. 'Education, through the city's three universities and other educational establishments, has breathed a new culture of youth into Liverpool. And young talented, energetic minds are tempted to stay on after their studies and have populated local businesses, providing a new driving force of achievement. Once again, Liverpool is at a turning point; its tide is turning and the city centre is being repopulated,' he says.

Dr Migos is excited that Liverpool is becoming a true 24-hour city, and observes that everywhere there is a spirit of euphoria, a sense of well-being. 'It was about time, too. Gone are the union troubles and the Militant political affiliations; gone too are the negative media damnations and the disparaging remarks by travel writers such as Bill Bryson, whose earlier observations about Liverpool focused on litter.'

In a bid to capture this new mood the school of architecture at JMU set its students the task of expressing the new vibrancy in the city in visual terms. Young minds, said the late Professor Quentin Hughes, see possibilities which, while not always entirely practicable, often provide a gift for those more mature minds who are responsible for the fabric of a city.

They were given the historic Mersey waterfront as the theme for exploring their ideas and proposals under the guidance of Dr Migos, a project that echoed the words of Professor Hughes, who was another of their mentors. In 1967 he wrote in the *Daily Telegraph,* pleading for the safeguarding of the impressive Albert Dock warehouses: 'In 30 years time, we could end up with somewhere like Venice; somewhere that was nice to live in.'

That dream and vision has actually been realised and his views on the concepts assembled by students almost 40 years later were prescient: 'Many are inspirational, the seeds which, given the right environment, may propagate. To aspire is the goal of life; achievement is often incidental.'

Dr Migos believes the *Re-animating the Waterfront* project exposed the young generation of architectural designers to a great challenge. It was a matter, he says, of raising to a higher plateau the level of aspiration and design for those studying at JMU's centre for architecture.'

It was summed up, reflects Dr Migos, by Richard Rodgers and Philip Gumuchdjian in the report *Cities For A Small Planet,* in 1967: '... Cities are the cradle of civilisation, the condensers and engines of our cultural development. Putting the culture of cities back on the political agenda is critical, for while they might be places where life is at its most precarious, cities can also fundamentally inspire ...'

'We believe our students did rise to the challenge and have delivered a 'vision' of an exciting and fantastic new direction for Liverpool. If it makes the purses of developers rattle with excitement, then it will have surpassed all our expectations.'

Then ... and now: the abandoned, silted up Canning Half-tide Dock in the early 1980s and today a bustling visitor attraction.

The Magnet that Makes People Stay
in the City that Can Drive Them Wild

Ken Martin is devoted to Liverpool in spite of itself

For close on five, frequently uproarious decades architect Ken Martin has been a ferocious campaigner for change in the unpredictable city that he holds dear, an infatuation nurtured often against his will while he raged against its idiosyncrasies. He harbours no qualms about this quasi-belligerent stance, but confesses he is permanently, almost fatally, attracted by the mystical element that makes Liverpool fizz.

This he acknowledges is awkward to pinpoint, but he considers it might be a celebration of its racial mélange, a heady confection of cultures and nationalities that has been baked with global ingredients, not the least the Celtic fringe that infuses the city's potpourri with an anarchic energy.

Ken has oft been regarded as a boisterous buckaroo in the cloistered confines of Liverpool's esteemed architect circles, his habitual outspoken Lancastrian bluntness regularly raising the blood pressures of folk reeling at his intemperance.

He concedes that he has relished his role as a media junkie but in mitigation can boast a string of worthy achievements: amongst others he restored the fabled Liverpool Playhouse theatre to its former glory and was largely responsible for the National Museums Liverpool's stunning, award-winning Conservation Centre that was elegantly restored from a bland former railway storehouse.

In contrast to the avuncular visage – he resembles movie mogul Sir Dickie Attenborough in mellow shadow – Martin is a fiery yet fervent man and he clearly embraces his hard won affection for Liverpool, plainly proud of its recent achievements, not the least the World Heritage tag. Although, ever the devil's advocate, he is inclined to raise a querulous eyebrow in this direction too, preferring to focus on the city's future potential rather than its cultural legacy.

Now 65, Ken Martin turned up in Liverpool as an architectural student in 1956 and apart from two wayward years where he plied his trade in York and Chester has stayed put, although he disdains the 'Adopted Scouser' refrain. For 20 years he taught architecture at the Liverpool Polytechnic and in his last year was a professor at John Moores University, a title he now and again likes to dust off.

'There is little doubt that Liverpool has been a difficult city to make things happen in, yet despite this it draws strangers like a magnet,' he declares.

He relished working on the world-famous Playhouse theatre – the oldest drama repertory venue in

Britain – and numerous other projects but is bemused to this day, that as an architect committed to the city he wasn't given the chance to handle a single brick out of the Albert Dock restoration project in the mid 1980s.

It is his firm conviction that cities afraid to evolve and be dynamic organisms will simply decline. Liverpool, he points out, had endured a period of such decline since World War II – and maybe he suggests as far back as the 1920s – with the population falling. 'It wasn't able to sustain a pattern of living in the city centre,' he observes. 'But the good news is that there is the stirring of a resurgence in city centre living. It hasn't yet reached the all important critical mass, and it may take another five or 10 years but it is happening.'

In terms of Liverpool's architectural future he steers back to his persuasions that the majority of buoyant and adventurous cities around the world are those that welcome tall buildings.

'My one real problem with the World Heritage ethics, even if the conservation values they embody are worthy, is that they could so easily be used as a policy document – albeit with the best intentions – to restrict such developments, akin to throwing out the baby with the bathwater.'

Ken Martin is audacious enough to remind the planners that Liverpool's wealth was built on entrepreneurial skills, thanks largely to the powerhouse of the river, never mind the added bonus of its stunning views; he raves about the general ambience of the place, the way the wind blows salty and fresh off the sea, the way the city was built on seven meandering hills, like Rome. 'Liverpool is an old mediaeval town with narrow streets and doesn't have a formal layout in the way of cities such as Paris. It grew irregularly and organically. And I believe there are opportunities for towers in various places that would – in my opinion – enhance it.

Ken Martin was born 65 years ago in the historic town of Lancaster, just to the south of the English Lake District. He came to Liverpool as an architecture student in 1956 and has never really left the area. He has engaged energetically in a love-fury relationship with his adopted city and worked on various projects that have helped change its image, although he would insist in only a modest way.

'If you design tall buildings that acknowledge and understand the other buildings around them, and they make some architectural reference to that, then you get a dialogue between buildings; and this makes for a fine city.

'If we are to build vibrant, modern cities we must have tall buildings in the right places, and naturally in scale with the city involved. This merely reflects the views of the Edwardians whose visionary approach is acknowledged by this World Heritage designation. They tackled what were then considered tall buildings: the Liver Building is a perfect example.

'The will to build high is an essential part of human nature: pyramids, cathedrals, towers; it is something we need to do. Perhaps it is a significant symbol about our humanity, an attempt to get nearer to God while shouting: 'We are here ... look at what we can do.'

Then he switches to the controversial arguments that rattle various cages when he declares that Liverpool has lacked confidence for far too long in architectural values, citing other cities around the world that have strode forward and upwards to demonstrate their positive outlook. 'We should have all manner of tall buildings on the waterfront as an expression of our vision, to exploit the vistas as much as demonstrate our technical abilities.'

He points out examples of cities that have recognised the need for a broader approach to building; similar American seaport cities like Boston and Baltimore where for decades they resisted proposals for tall buildings, anxious to retain their

Concept for the Paradise Street Project that will transform Liverpool city centre.

Georgian architectural splendour. As a result they declined catastrophically, believes Ken, who explains that when they changed their minds the cities rose again, and now the older buildings nestle almost sympathetically with the tall towers, an integral part of the quality of those places.

'And I think we have better architects than the Americans, hugely creative people of world renown such as Will Alsop. I am a supporter of his Cloud project in Liverpool because it is imaginative and will be a significant building on the Pier Head.'

Today Ken Martin is the active principal of KE Martin Architects based in Mathew Street in Liverpool's legendary Cavern Street Quarter, practising his technical – and debating – skills on various projects.

There in the narrow, cobbled streets that helped spawn Liverpool's musical heritage of Mersey Beat and the Beatles, he also runs one of the city's independent and more eclectic art galleries. The View provides a platform – and salesroom – for young painters and sculptors who are the new generation of artists that Ken is keen to encourage, another of his passions.

'Of course I have this ongoing love affair with Liverpool, in spite of my seeming fury at its apparent disorder. The great thing about bringing friends to the city – especially architects – is that they have a preconception, an image historically muddied by the media to an extent; they expect a down-at-heel city, a collection of boring industrial old piles blotting the landscape. They are invariably surprised at the quality of the architecture.'

Ken is thrilled at the changes wrought in Liverpool in recent times, after so long regarded as a difficult city, downtrodden and looked upon by the rest of the nation as the 'end of the road; the end of the motorway network; the end of the railway lines'; striving to support a declining port – no matter the inaccuracy of that belief – and with everyone content to write it off as a dead loss.

'It is marvellous that Liverpool's time has come again. What we have to do in the next 10 to 15 years is to capitalise on that and turn it into a truly remarkable city for the 21st century. The 10 years after European Capital of Culture in 2008 will be the ones that matter.'

He urges people to take a look at cities like Barcelona and Bilbao – that suffered through the same economic and social frailties that dogged Liverpool for so long – and he promises they will send your spirits soaring.

He agrees that they have in many ways absolved themselves of the past, while saluting it, and invested in modern, striking – and tall – buildings.

'I would like to see Liverpool filled with such conspicuous and dazzling structures, designed by creative architects and using the finest of materials and good workmanship. Liverpool deserves that kind of effort so that it can become a truly cosmopolitan city, one of considerable substance and style.'

'... the song that was soon on the lips of every Scouser from Timbuktu to Toronto ... was first unleashed in the Wash House ...'

Peter McGovern

see essay page 62

Turning Liverpool's City Centre into a 21st Century Paradise

There was a mood of subdued excitement pervading the room when three of the world's most eminent urban designers met in Liverpool three years ago to discuss the plans for an inner city regeneration scheme that has been dubbed as probably one of the most crucial in the city's history.

Sir Terry Farrell, Rafael Vinoly and Cesar Pelli joined architects from Building Design Partnership and other members of the 'master planning team' to mull over ideas proposed by Grosvenor, the Duke of Westminster's property company, and to consider them in the context of the city's important waterfront and how the project might impact on Liverpool's designation as a World Heritage site.

They talked about retaining – as far as practicable – the existing street pattern, buildings of historic or architectural interest and existing public open space, and suggested that existing views and historic buildings be kept, with new views, walkways and buildings created around them, to fashion a truly 21st century city centre. In addition, the Grosvenor team looked at the principles of creating distinct areas or 'quarters' that would respond to the physical characteristics of the site and surrounding areas and would provide a broad range of shopping, leisure and residential activities, to forge variety in the character of the streets and open spaces.

After those early workshops Cesar Pelli worked as an advisor with the team drawing up the masterplan. Like everyone else involved in the £750 million redevelopment, tagged the Paradise Street Project, he is delighted that by 2008 it will have transformed 42 acres at the heart of the city, an outcome that city council chief Sir David Henshaw says will be one of the

seminal moments in Liverpool's regeneration. 'There has been a tendency in Liverpool in the past to see the glass as half empty. Here in the city we are now in a position to witness one of the largest city centre developments taking place anywhere in Europe. It is astonishing evidence of the re-emergence of Liverpool's nerve. This transformation will take people's breath away and confirm our place on the world map of dynamic cities,' he remarked.

Talks about the development potential of the area around Paradise Street and Chavasse Park have been going on for about a decade, but it was only in March 2000 that the property firm Grosvenor was chosen as the preferred developer. Then, only weeks before UNESCO announced that Liverpool was to be recognised for its architectural legacy with a World Heritage listing, their plans were approved with huge public support.

Grosvenor's chief executive Stephen Musgrave has described the scheme as one of the most exciting and ambitious ever undertaken by the group and he predicted that the massive workload will be virtually completed by the time Liverpool is throwing a party to celebrate being European Capital of Culture in 2008.

The UK's deputy prime minister John Prescott has hailed Liverpool's 'renaissance', claiming that a 'quiet revolution' had taken place in recent years with new forms

Rod Holmes considers the 'eye sores' that will soon be demolished.

of wealth creation replacing the factories and shipyards of the Industrial Revolution, a period that gave Liverpool an international reputation and influence. He commented: 'Our cities are back and the reasons are simple. They remain the centres for wealth creation, trade and culture. The old industrial economy may have gone, but cities are as important as ever.'

Liverpool city council leader Mike Storey believes that the transformation of the city is staggering. 'The new Liverpool is about to happen, and we can't wait.'

As the project moves forward cranes will dominate Liverpool's skyline. Thirty new buildings will pop up as architects produce exciting, trailblazing designs surrounded by new public spaces. A revamped Chavasse Park will emerge, graced with pavilions and a terrace from which visitors and citizens alike can view the city's spectacular, world-class waterfront.

The Paradise Street project director Rod Holmes explained that two flagship department stores are to open, along with dozens of other shops and hotels, a new bus station and a cinema. By 2008 six new, bustling shopping districts will have sprung up, turning the city into one of Europe's leading shopping destinations. He added: 'The 42-acre site is the equivalent of 21 football pitches and will restore Liverpool to the top of the champions' league for shopping and entertainment.' Apart from Grosvenor's own investment, the project has attracted other international investors and banks.

In the long term, says Mr Holmes, this is one of the most important joint public-private sector endeavours in the UK, and arguably Europe, that will benefit the whole of Liverpool and help bring prosperity to the region with jobs, houses, more businesses, more choices and more opportunities for everyone, more visitors from Britain, Europe and the world, and a cleaner, safer, pleasanter and more exciting environment.

Council leader Storey says the Paradise Street Project is a symbol of Liverpool's future: 'While we have admiration for our splendid cultural and architectural legacy we have a burning ambition to embrace the future.'

'Liverpool is the only city you can walk around with
the chief executive and people will stop him in the street
and tell him how to run the place, sometimes affably,
occasionally forcibly but always with an 'informed' passion.
I've never seen this in any other city in Britain,
and it is a mark of the intense belief in Liverpool that fuels
the outspoken directness of its citizens.

I am proud to be from Merseyside and World Heritage
status gives people in the city – and elsewhere – a fresh
opportunity to raise their awareness of its fantastic history
and heritage: a chance to remind them how lucky we are.'

Brenda Smith

Brenda Smith is group managing director of Ascent Media, a subsidiary of the giant US Liberty Media
and deputy chairman of Granada Television. She sits on the boards of the North West Development Agency,
the Liverpool Culture Company, Liverpool Vision and the Mersey Partnership.

Guy Woodland was born in Karachi and has lived and worked extensively in Australia, Pakistan, Ethiopia, Portugal, Brazil and the UK. He studied at Blackpool and Fylde College, earning a diploma in professional photography. He owns

liverpoolphotos.com, an online global picture resource, and operates internationally as a photographer. He is a co-founder and director of *cities500* and an associate of *Barge Pole Press,* an international collaboration of writers, photographers and graphic designers. He has previously published the popular photographic studies *Shed KM, The Life of Chester, The Life of the Gateway Theatre* and *The Life of Liverpool* as well as a profile of the sculptor Stephen Broadbent. He has also published *Liverpool: Waterfront,* a photographic essay study, and a collection of Mike McCartney's photographic memories in the critically acclaimed *Mike McCartney's Liverpool Life.* As a director of *Garlic Press* he was also co-author of *Liverpool: The First 1,000 Years, The Grand National Quiz Book* and *Cross the Mersey.*

Lew Baxter is a writer and journalist stirred by clearly defined Celtic passions, stemming from a provenance connected to both Scotland and Ireland. And he lives in Wales. Currently heading up the UK based *Action Media* agency, he is co-founder of *cities500,* the international publishing project, and an associate of *Barge Pole Press,* a worldwide collaboration of award winning writers, photographers and graphic designers. He has over 30 years' experience as a journalist, writing variously for the *Sunday Times* and *Sunday Mirror, Daily Telegraph,* the *Scotsman, China Daily,* the *Shanghai Star* and the *Hong Kong Standard* amongst others. He has also edited a range of newspapers and magazines, including the arts focussed *Scene Out.* He spent seven years in China where he was latterly bureau chief of *Sino Media Limited,* a multinational media agency, and consultant editor

for the multilingual weekly magazine *Beijing Review.* He also worked as a senior consultant editor at the *Xinhua News Agency* in Beijing. His books include *The Fool on the Hill* and *The Tragical History Tour.* He also worked with Guy Woodland on *Liverpool: Waterfront,* contributing the main essay.